The Magic Tales

Portraits of Enchantment

In the quiet moments of life, beneath the surface of the everyday, a world of enchantment awaits. Within the corners of time, amidst the laughter, tears, and contemplative gazes, stories unfold, tales are woven, and magic is found. These are the stories that dance through the lens of a camera, captured in a fraction of a second yet etched into eternity.

Welcome to "The Magic Tales: Portraits of Enchantment," a collection of the moments that have touched my soul, stirred my imagination, and filled my heart with wonder. This book is not merely a compilation of photographs; it's a journey into the lives, emotions, and dreams of the people who have crossed my path and allowed me to capture a piece of their essence.

As a photographer, I've been privileged to explore my soul through my camera's viewfinder. From bustling city streets to tranquil rural landscapes, from the faces of strangers to the expressions of loved ones, each image is a testament to the beauty and complexity of our existence. It is my humble attempt to reveal the stories that reside within each frame, stories that may have remained untold without the magic of photography.

These portraits are not just frozen moments; they are invitations to delve into the lives and experiences of those who have shared their stories with me. Each photograph represents a fragment of time, a glimpse into the extraordinary within the ordinary, an exploration of the soul behind the face.

"The Magic Tales" is an ode to the enchantment that surrounds us daily, waiting to be discovered if we take a moment to look. It is a testament to the power of photography to transport us to worlds unseen, to touch our hearts, and to inspire our own stories.

I invite you to turn the pages of this book, to immerse yourself in the enchantment of these portraits, and to find your own magic within the tales they tell. May they remind us all that, in the simplest of moments, there is beauty, in the faces of others, there is connection, and in the stories of everyday life, there is enchantment.

With gratitude and wonder,

Nickos IV

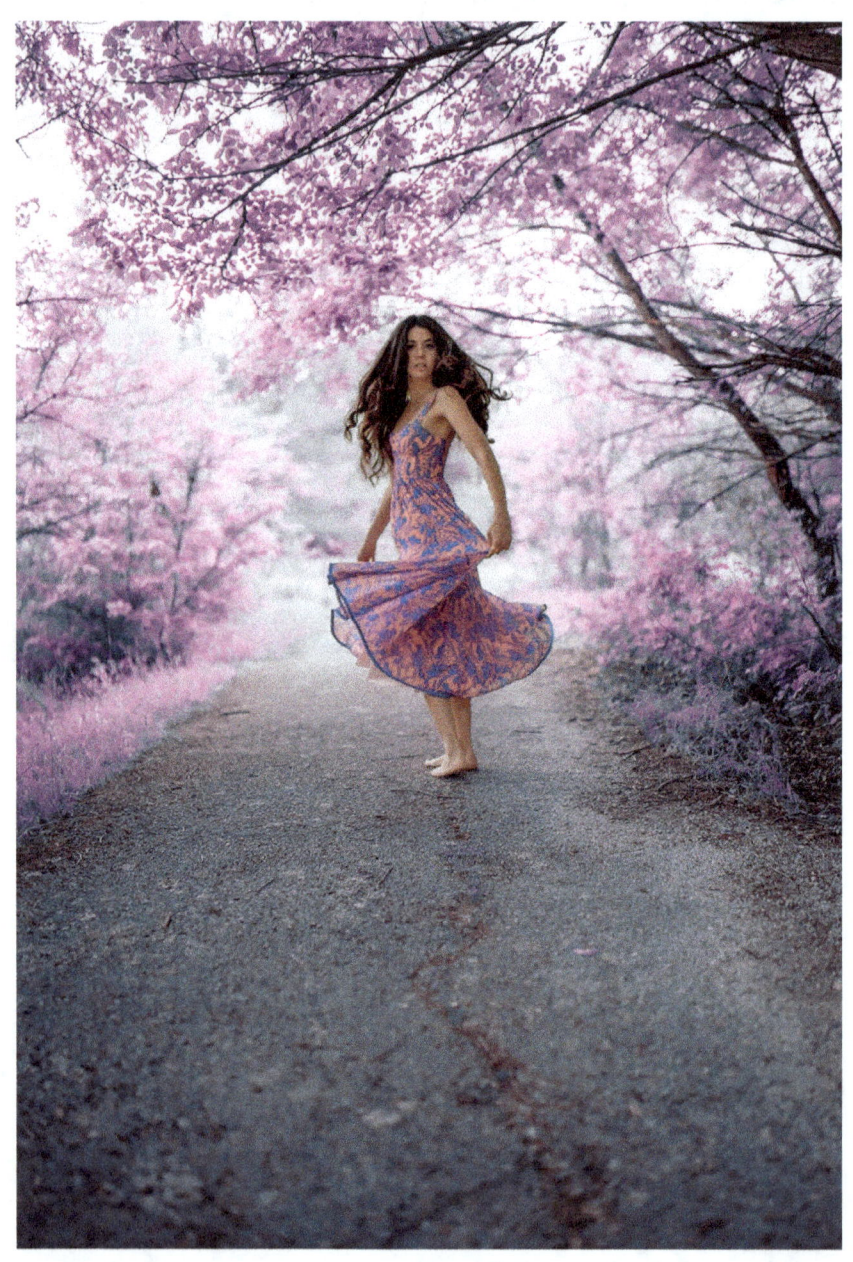

"When words become unclear, I shall focus with photographs. When images become inadequate, I shall be content with silence."
— Ansel Adams

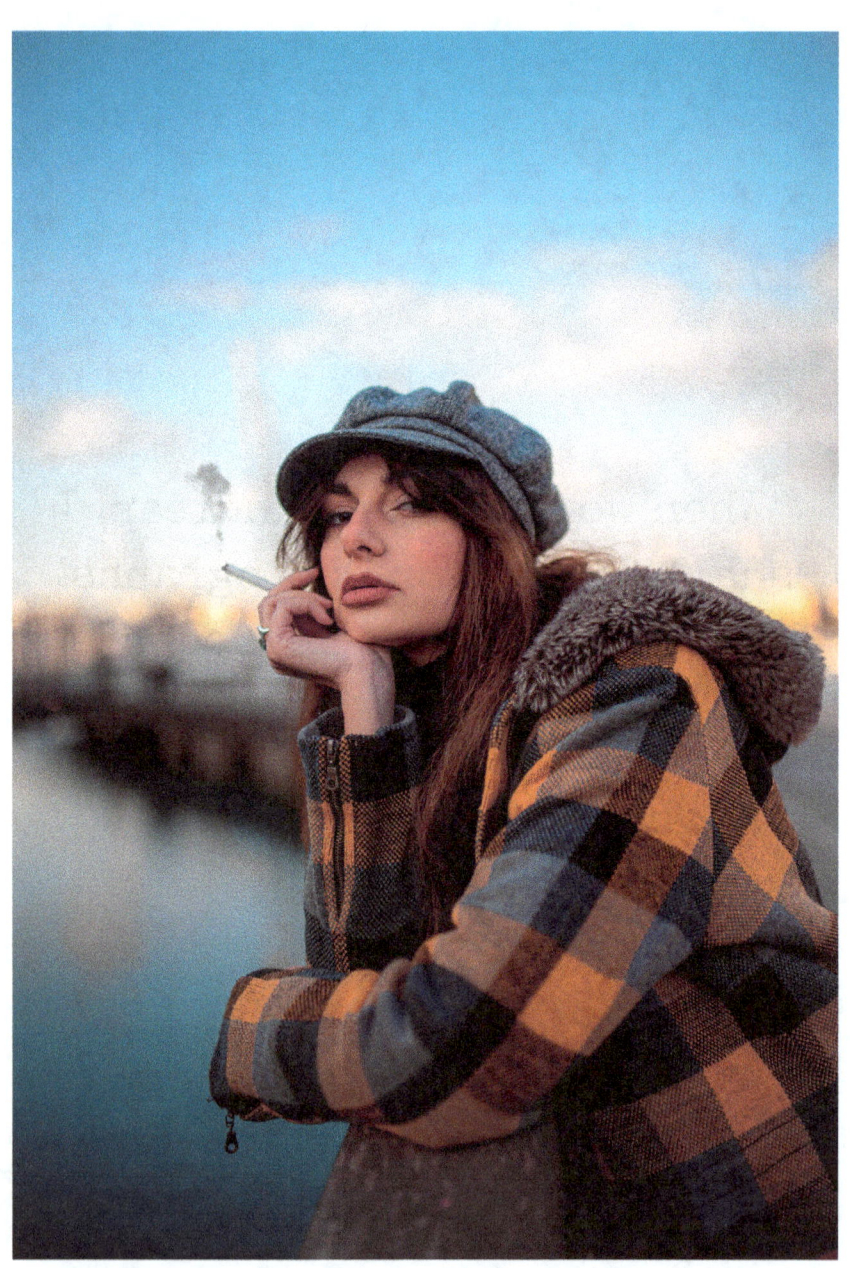

"In photography there is a reality so subtle that it becomes more real than reality."
— Alfred Stieglitz

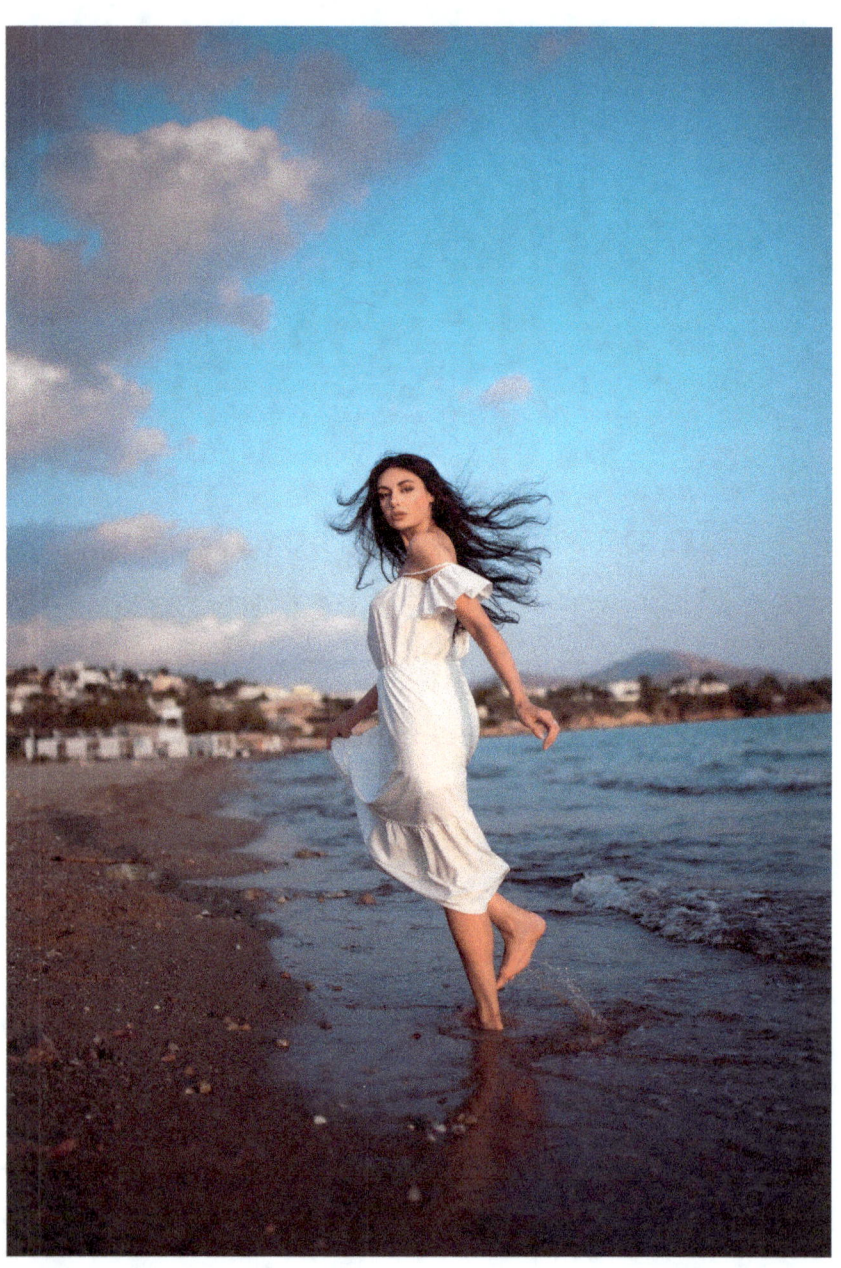

"There is one thing the photograph must contain, the humanity of the moment."
— Robert Frank

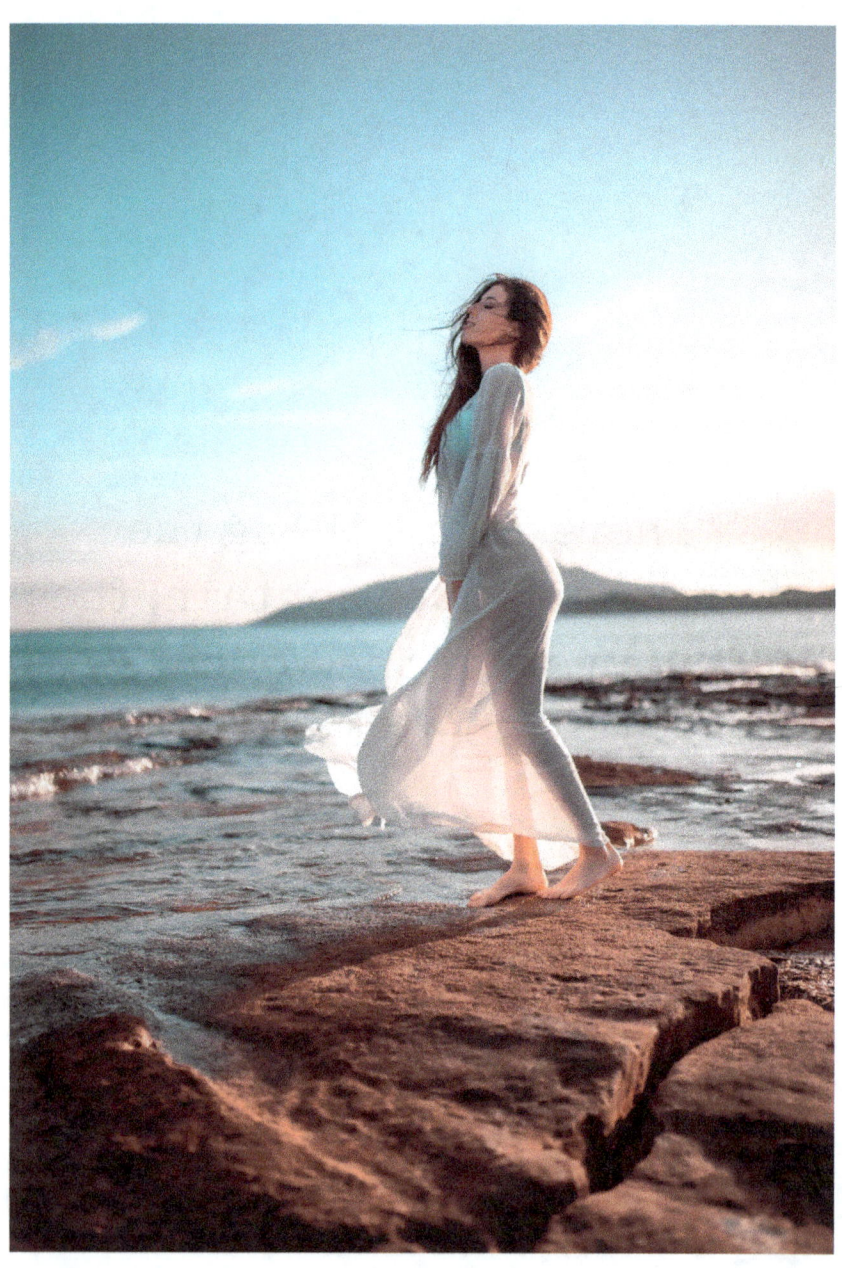

"Taking an image, freezing a moment, reveals how rich reality truly is."
— Anonymous

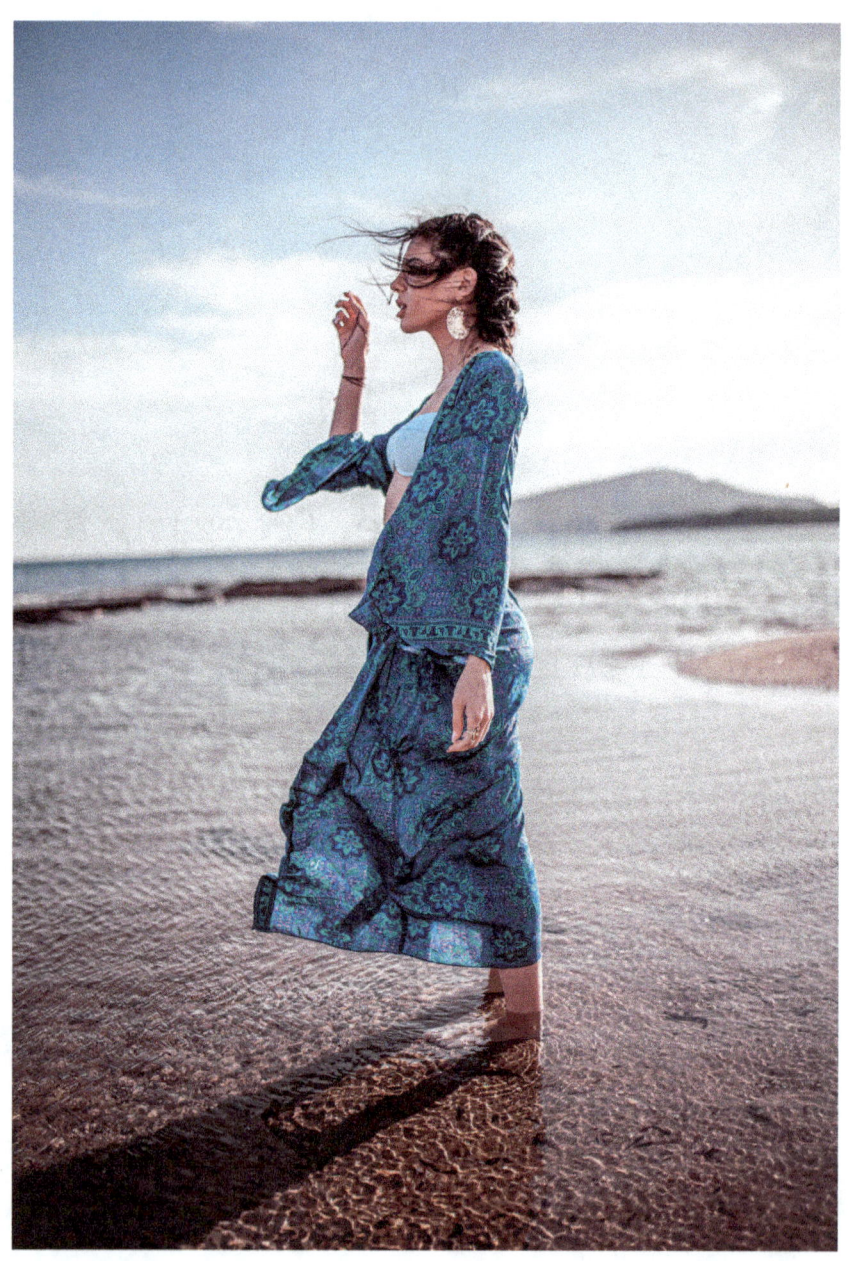

Photography is a way of feeling, of touching, of loving. What you have caught on film is captured forever... It remembers little things, long after you have forgotten everything."
— Aaron Siskind

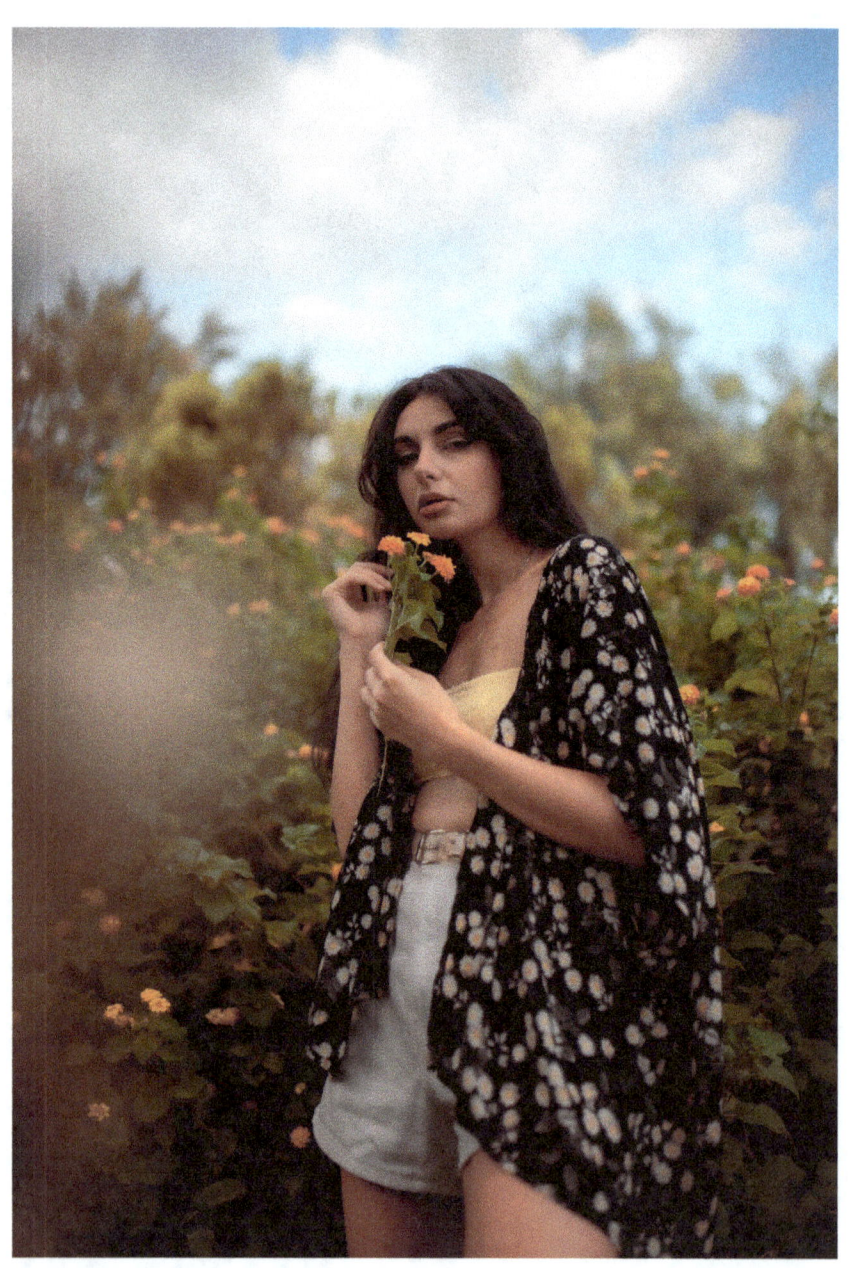

"When I have a camera in my hand, I know no fear."
— Alfred Eisenstaedt

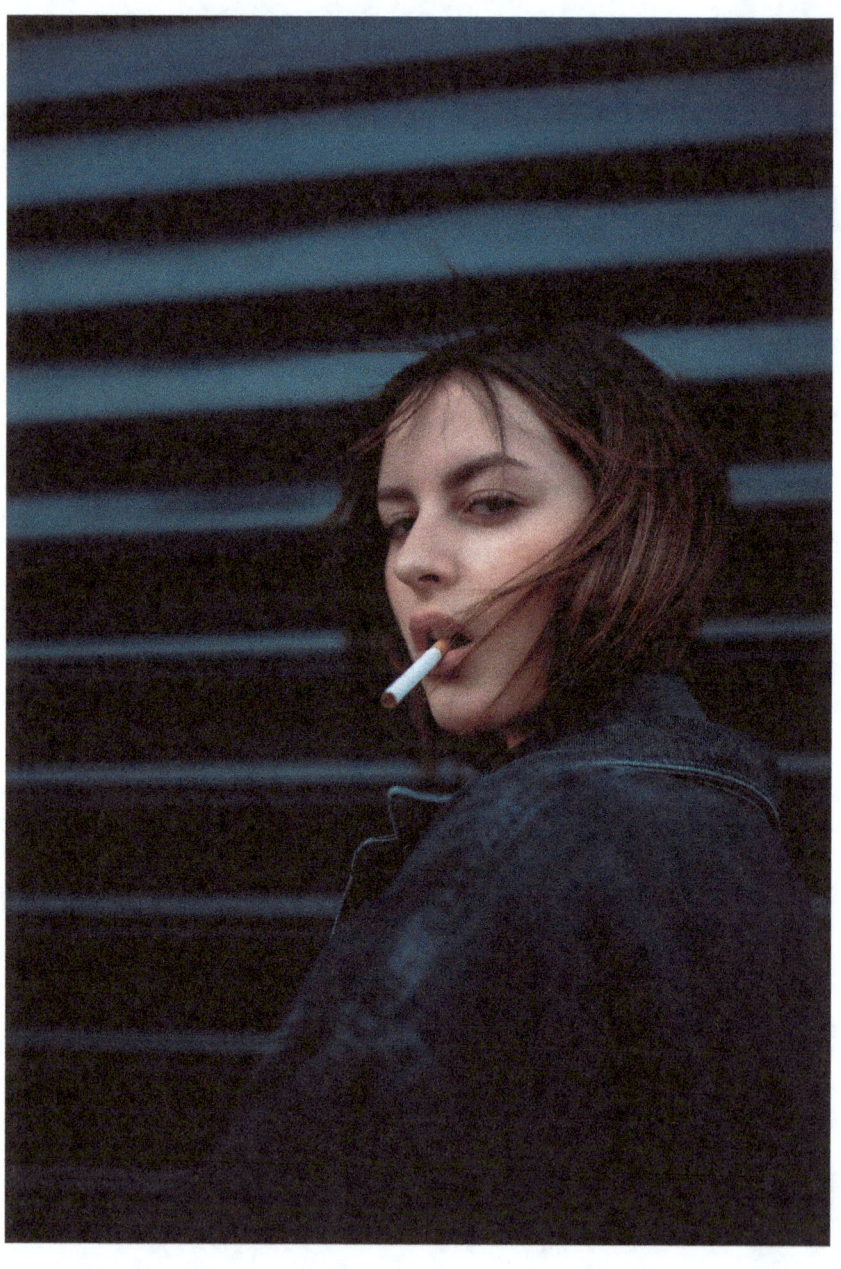

"We are making photographs to understand what our lives mean to us."
— Ralph Hattersley

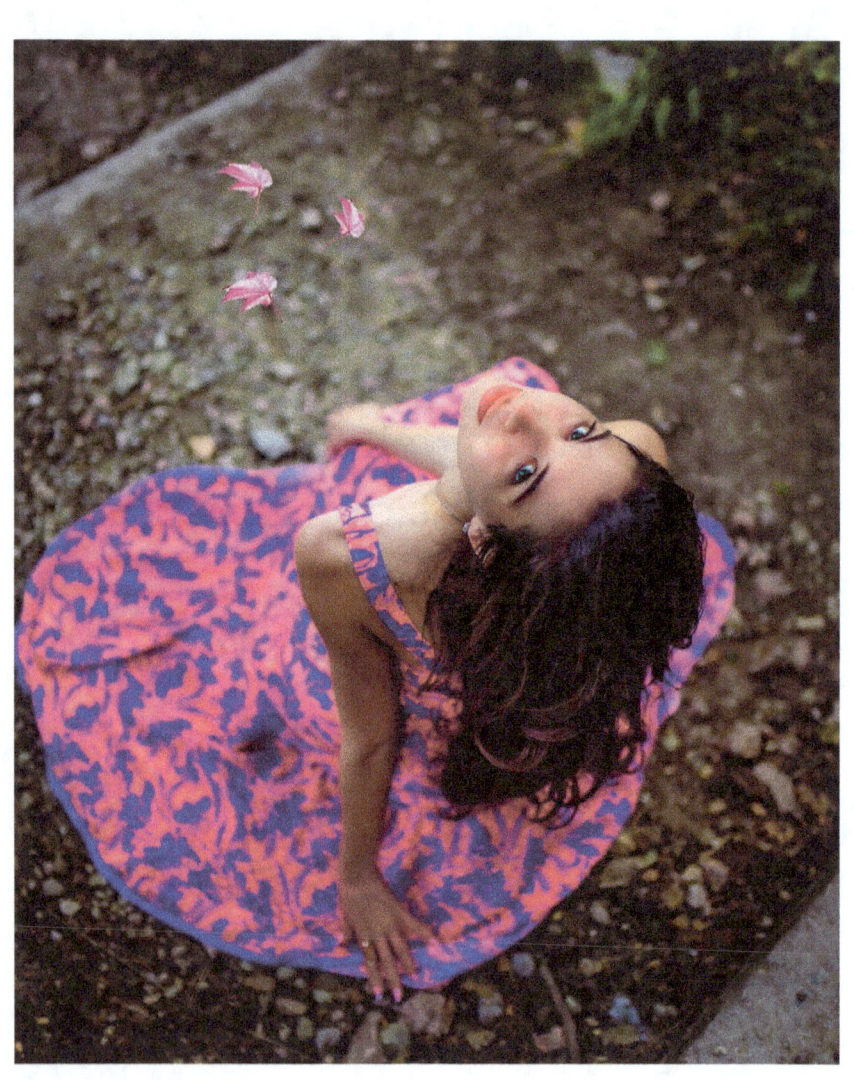

"A thing that you see in my pictures is that I was not afraid to fall in love with these people."
— Annie Leibovitz

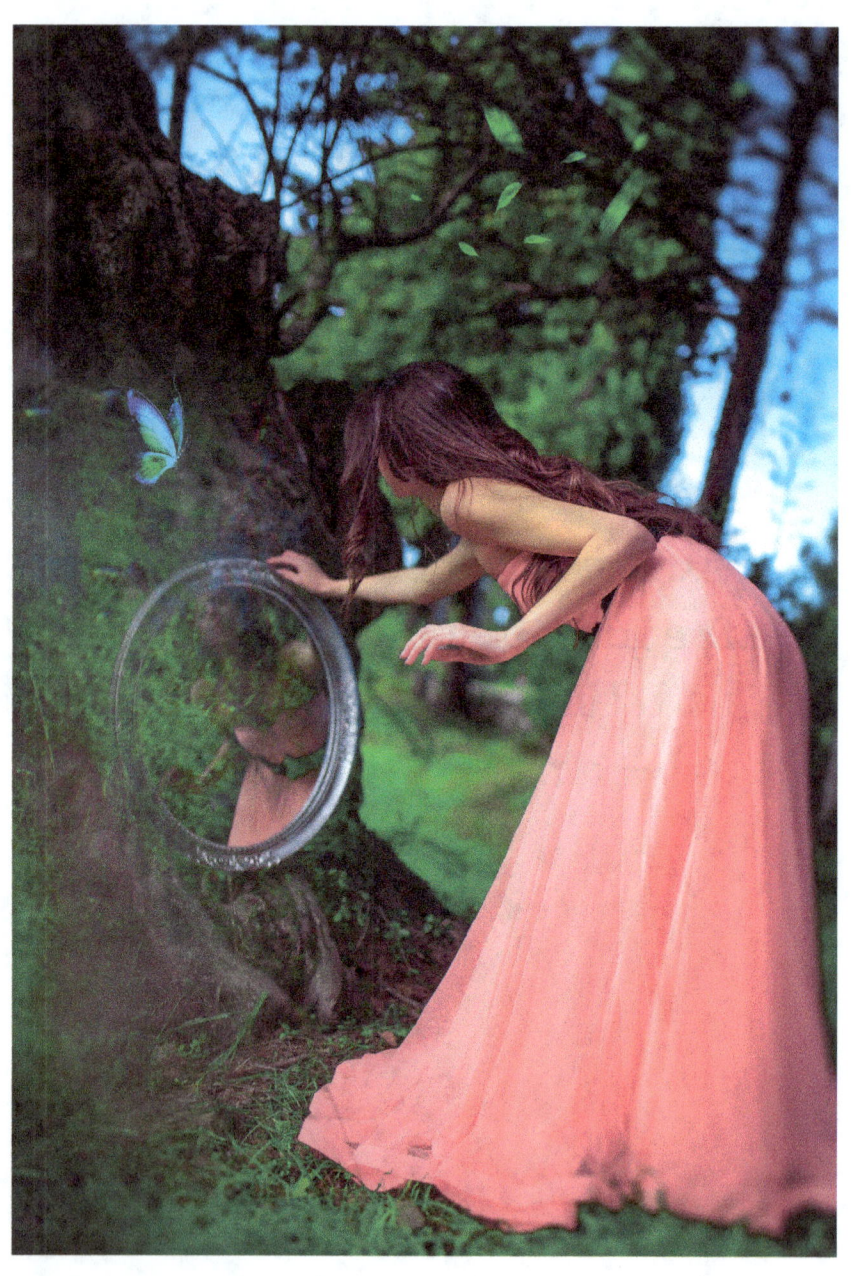

"You don't take a photograph.
You ask quietly to borrow it."
— Unknown

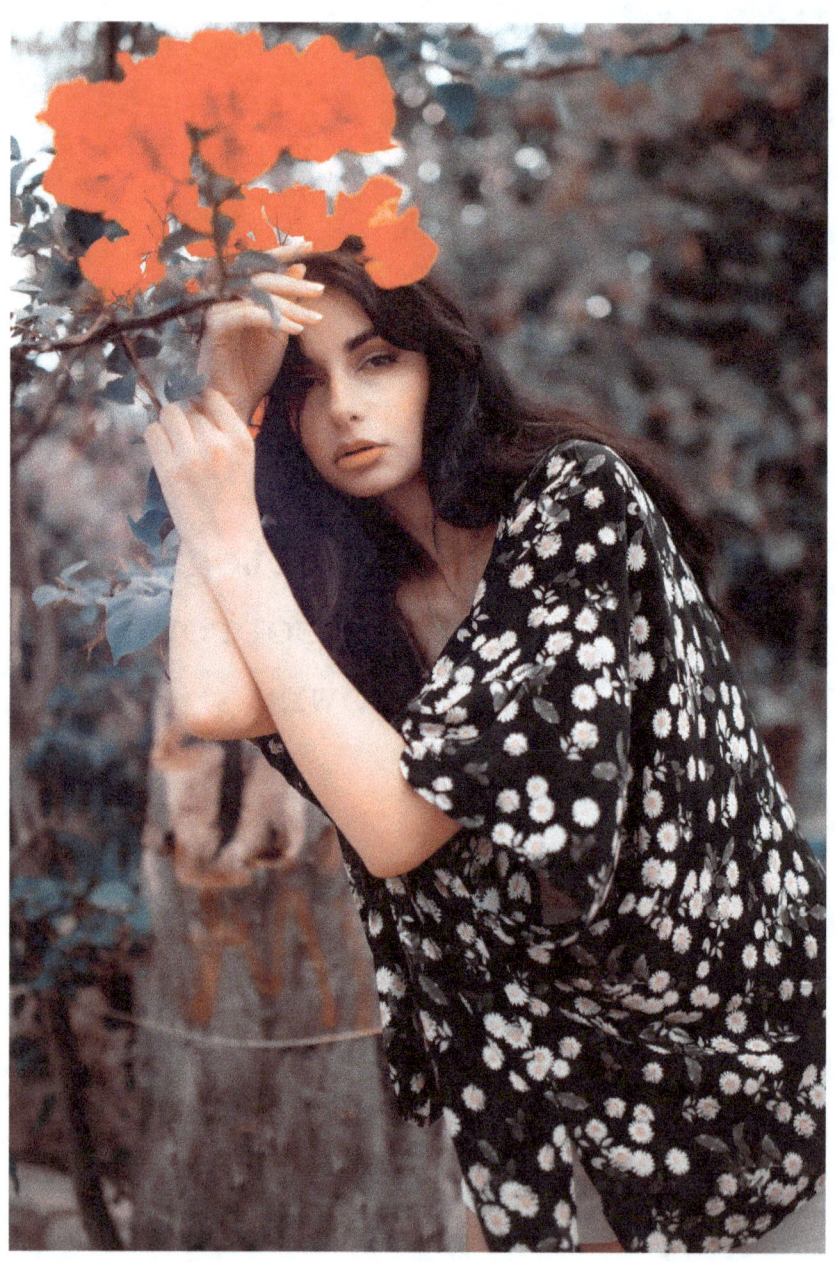

"Photography for me is not looking, it's feeling. If you can't feel what you're looking at, then you're never going to get others to feel anything when they look at your pictures."
— Don McCullin

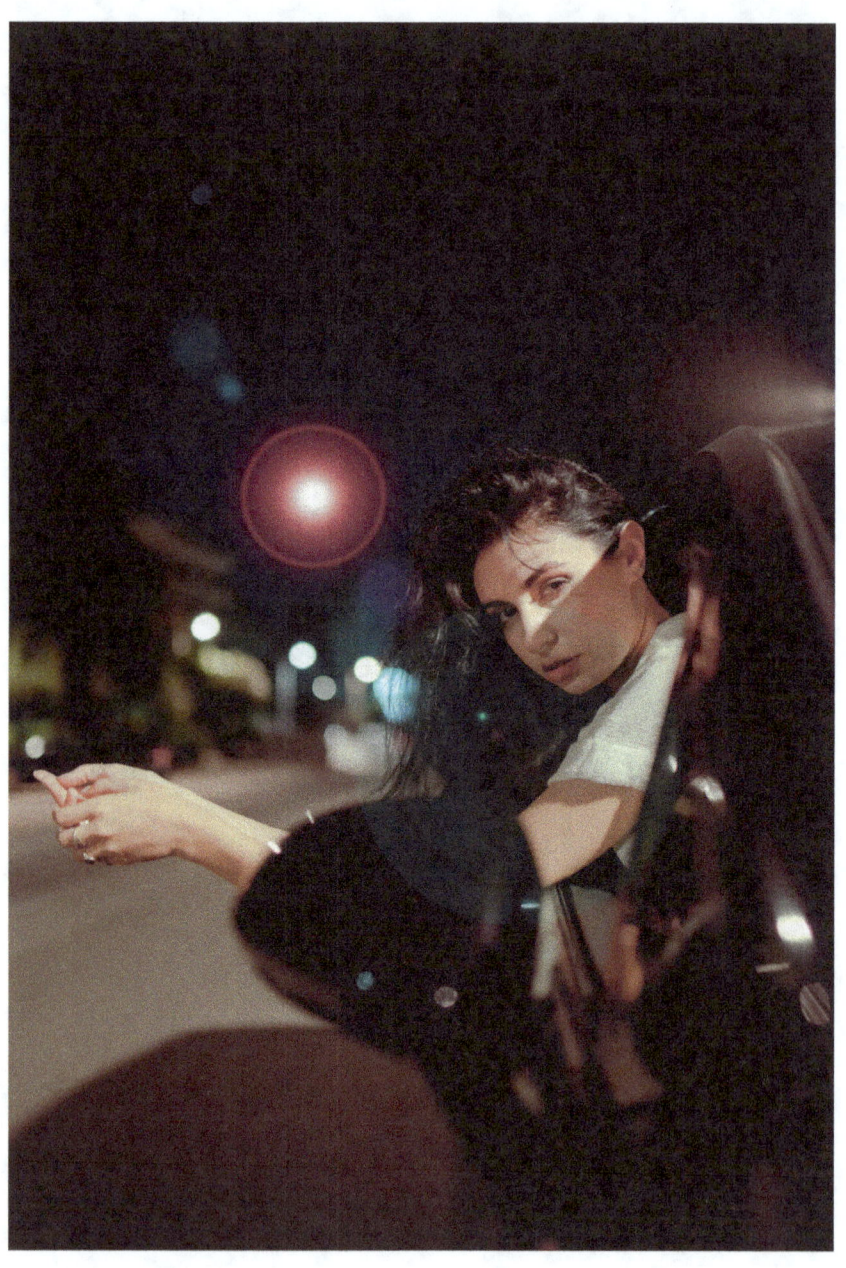

"If it excites me, there is a good chance it will make a good photograph."
— Ansel Adams

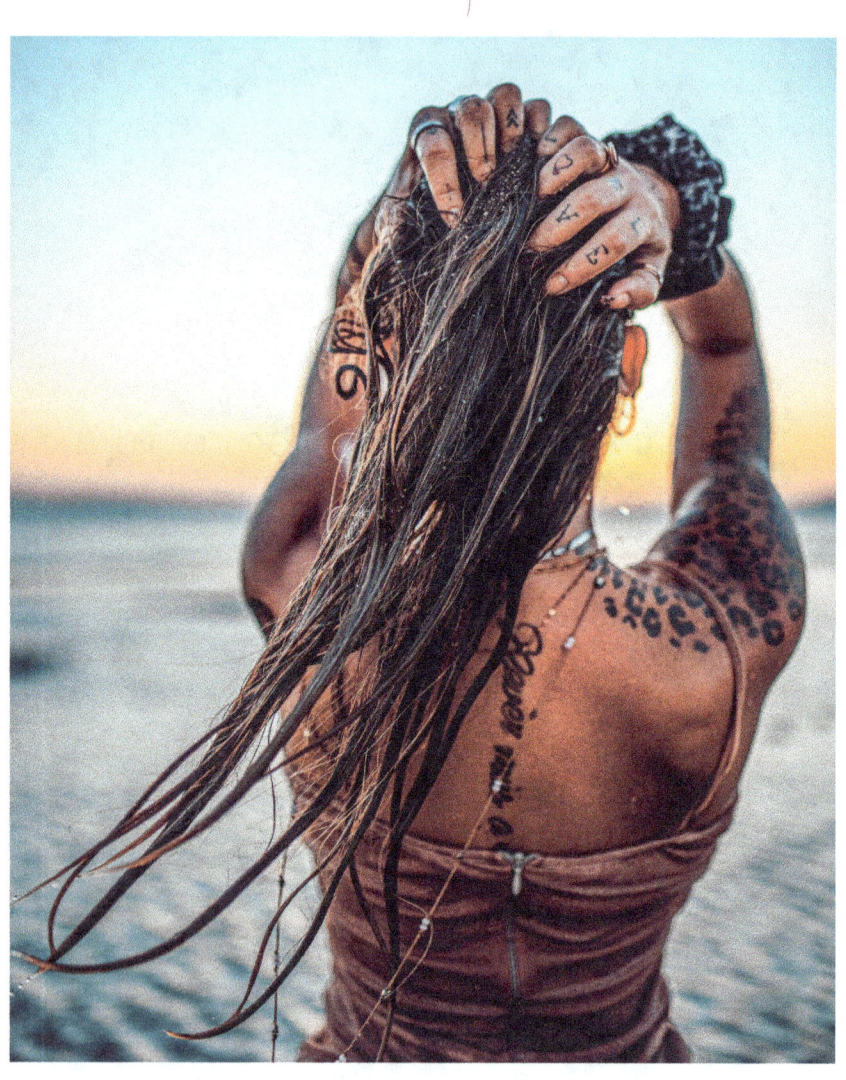

"The best thing about a picture is that it never changes, even when the people in it do."
— Andy Warhol

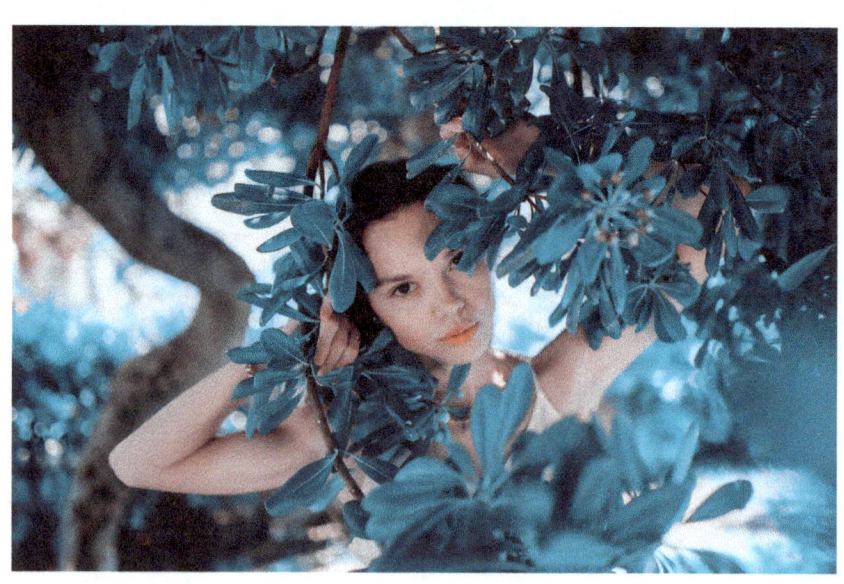

"A portrait is not made in the camera but on either side of it."
— Edward Steichen

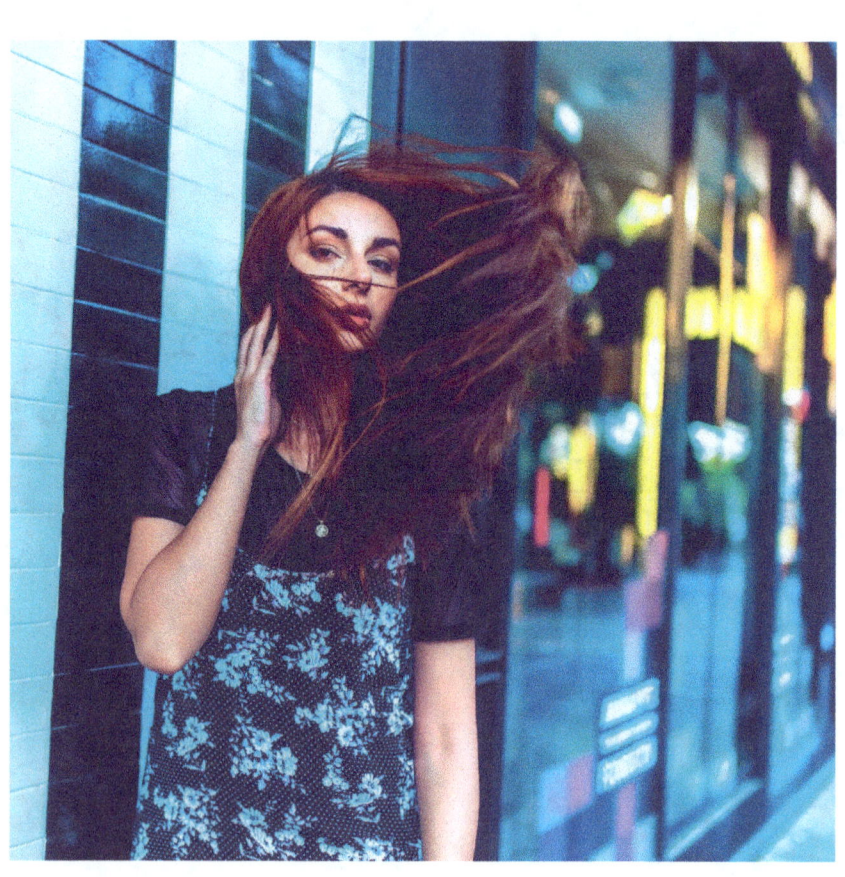

"What makes photography a strange invention is that its primary raw materials are time and light."
— John Berger

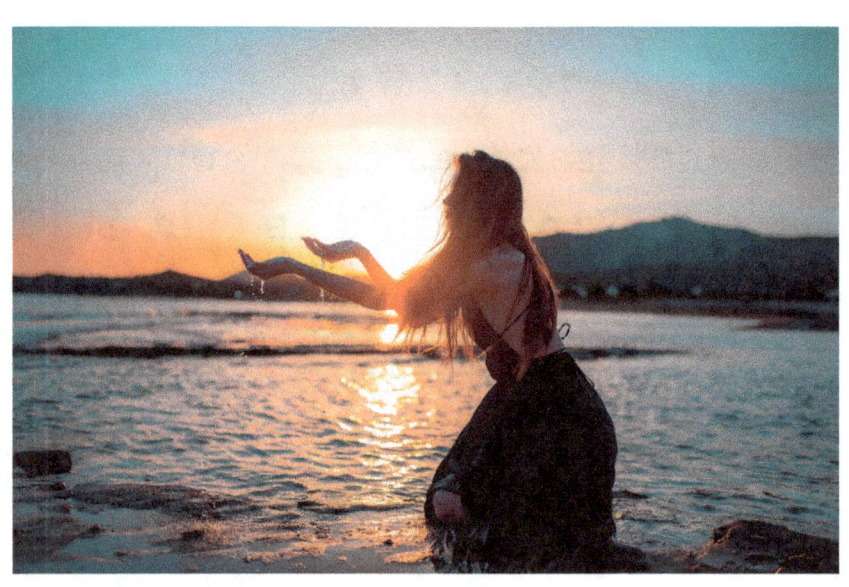

"To me, photography is an art of observation. It's about finding something interesting in an ordinary place... I've found it has little to do with the things you see and everything to do with the way you see them."
— Elliott Erwitt

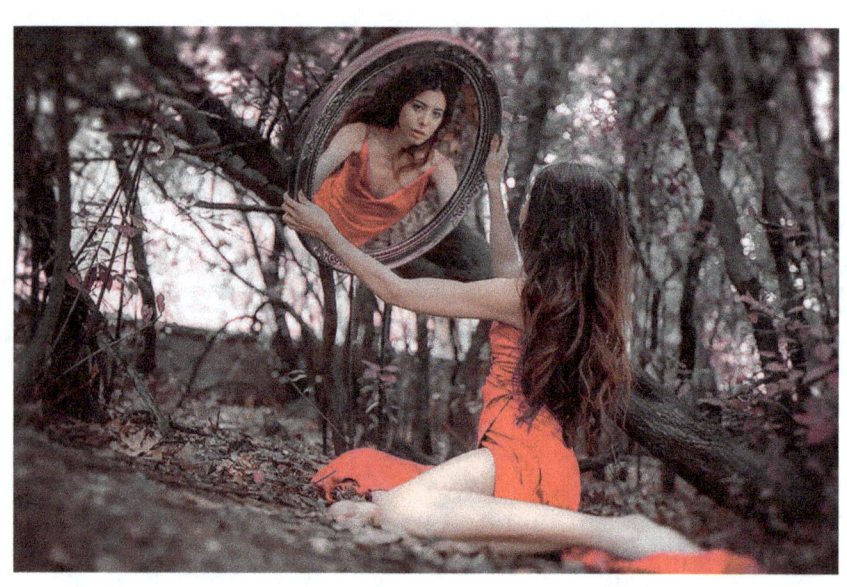

"The picture that you took with your camera is the imagination you want to create with reality."
— Scott Lorenzo

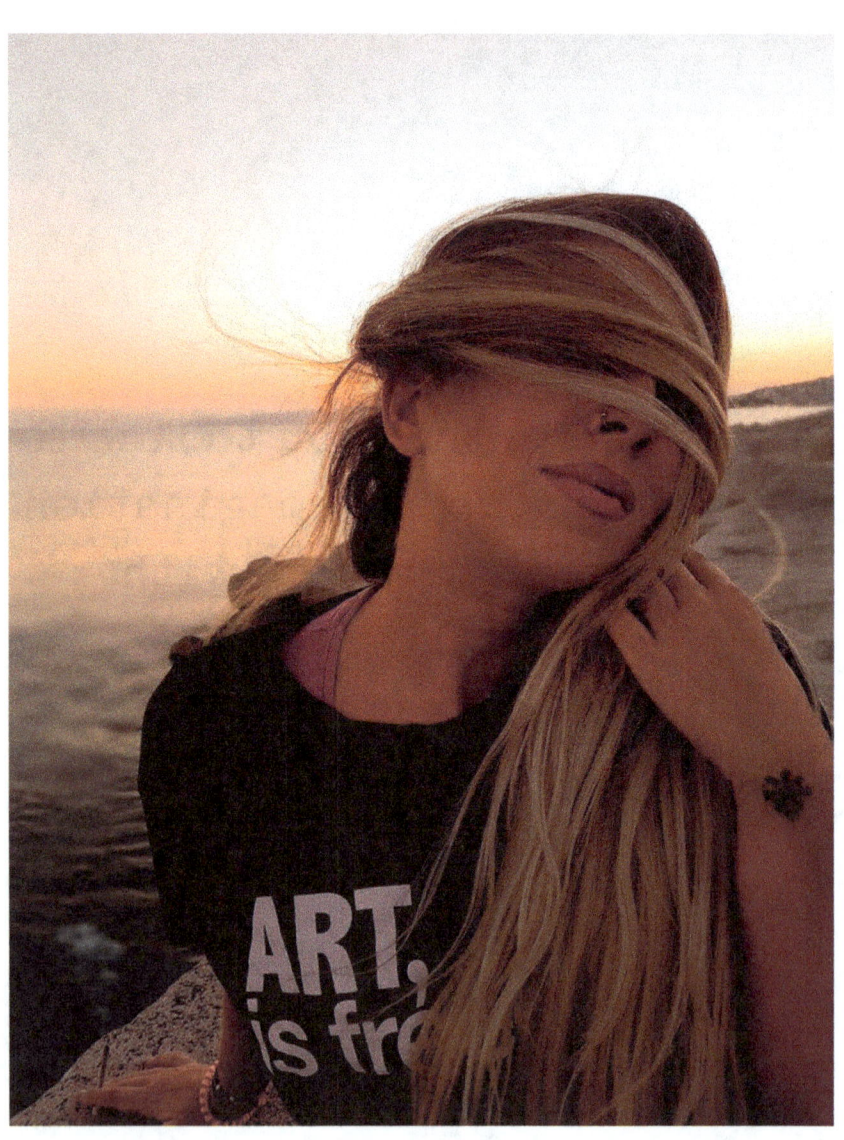

"If the photographer is interested in the people in front of his lens, and if he is compassionate, it's already a lot. The instrument is not the camera but the photographer."
— Eve Arnold

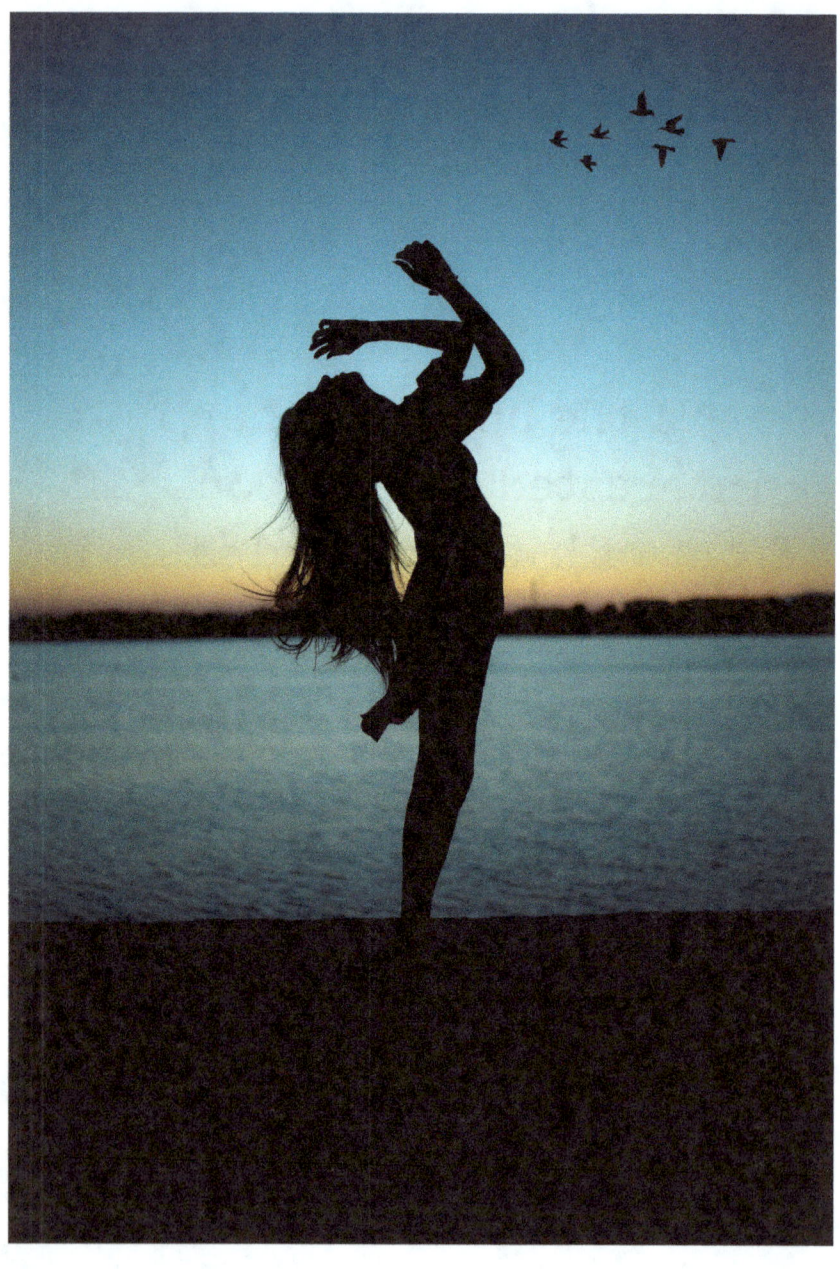

"A tear contains an ocean. A photographer is aware of the tiny moments in a persons life that reveal greater truths."
— Anonymous

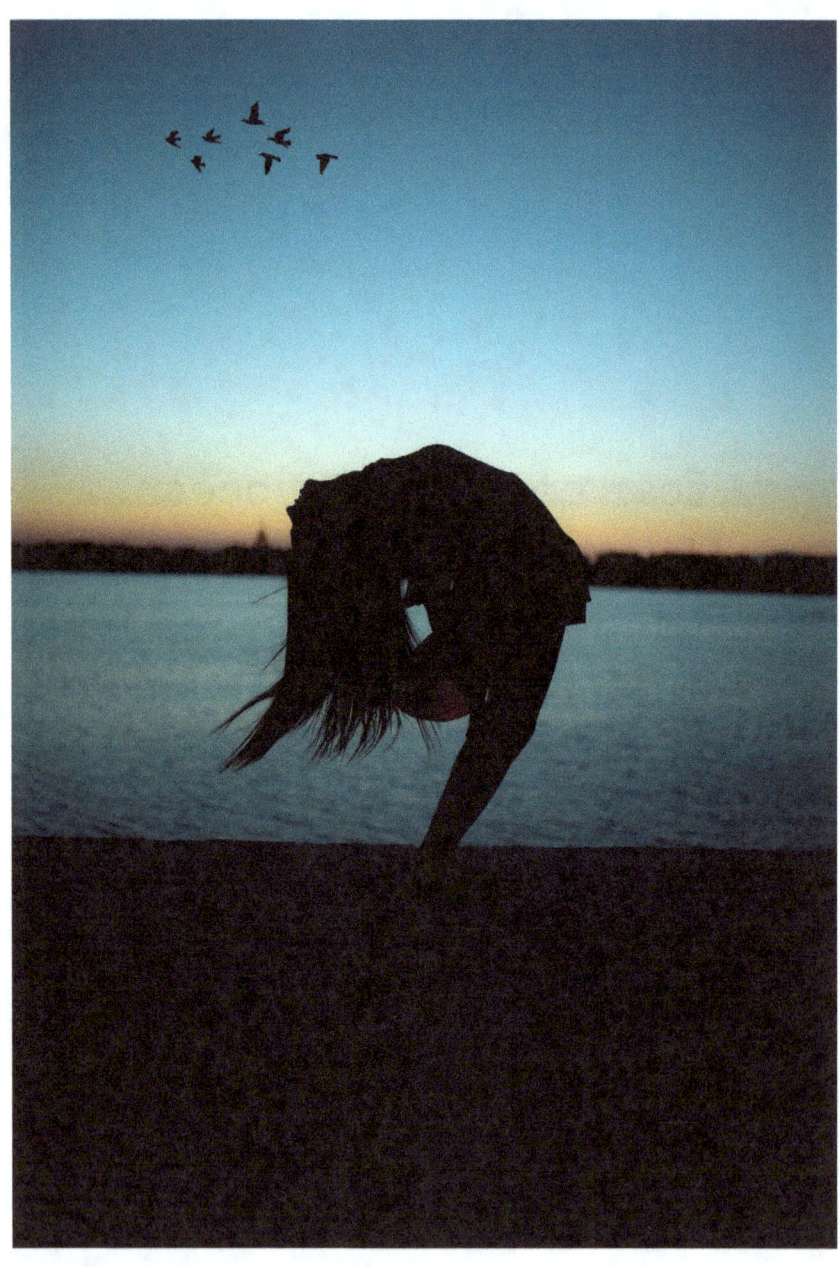

"The camera is an instrument
that teaches people how to see
without a camera."
— Dorothea Lange

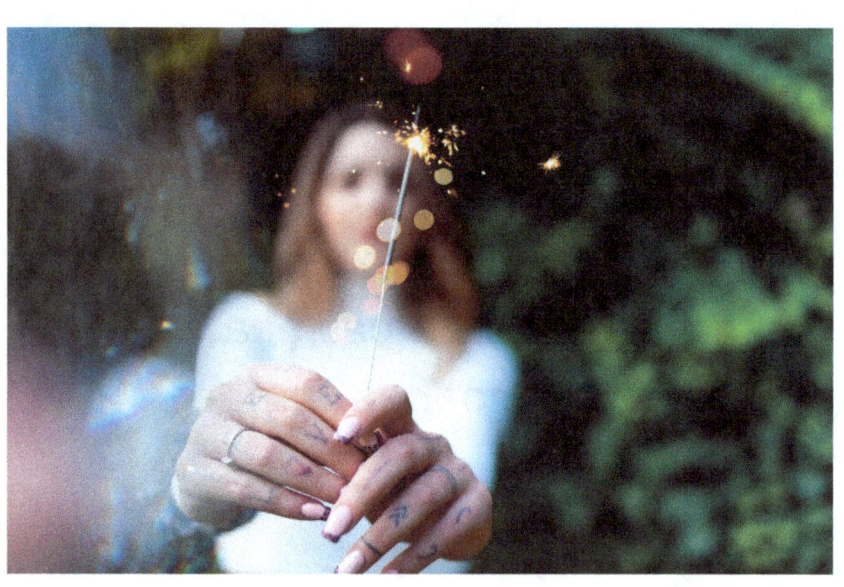

"I don't trust words. I trust pictures."
— Gilles Peress

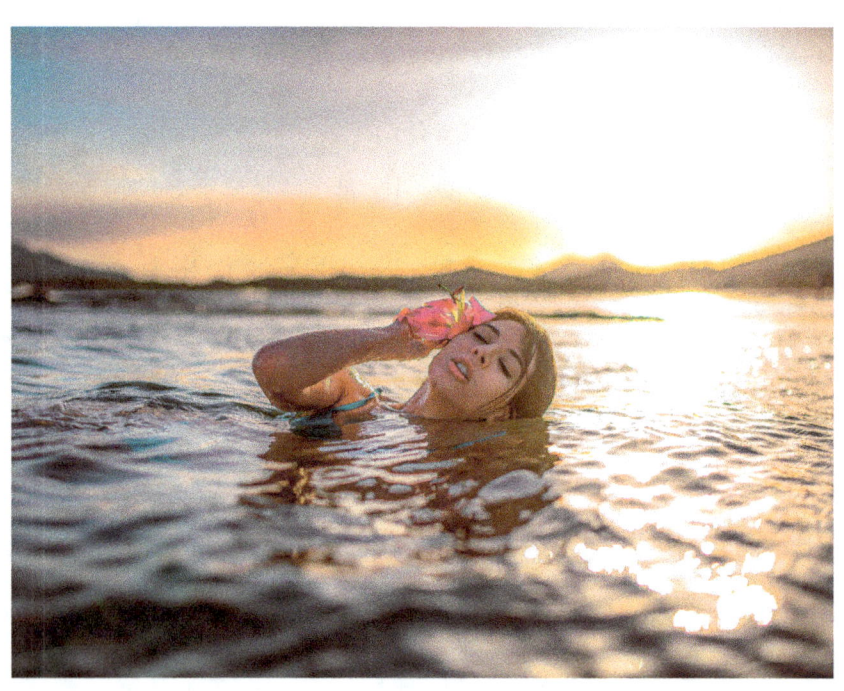

"I really believe there are things nobody would see if I didn't photograph them."
— Diane Arbus

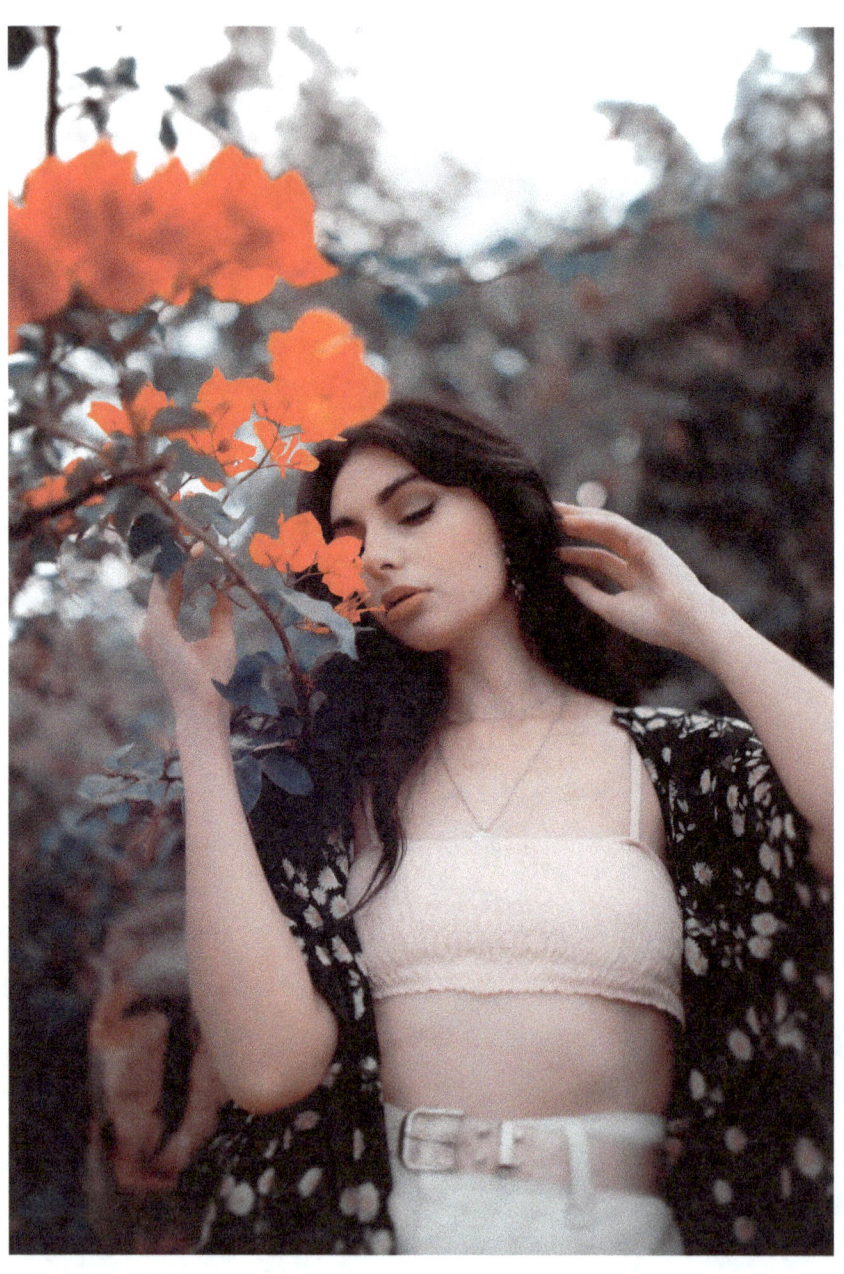

"Taking pictures is savoring
life intensely, every hundredth
of a second."
— Marc Riboud

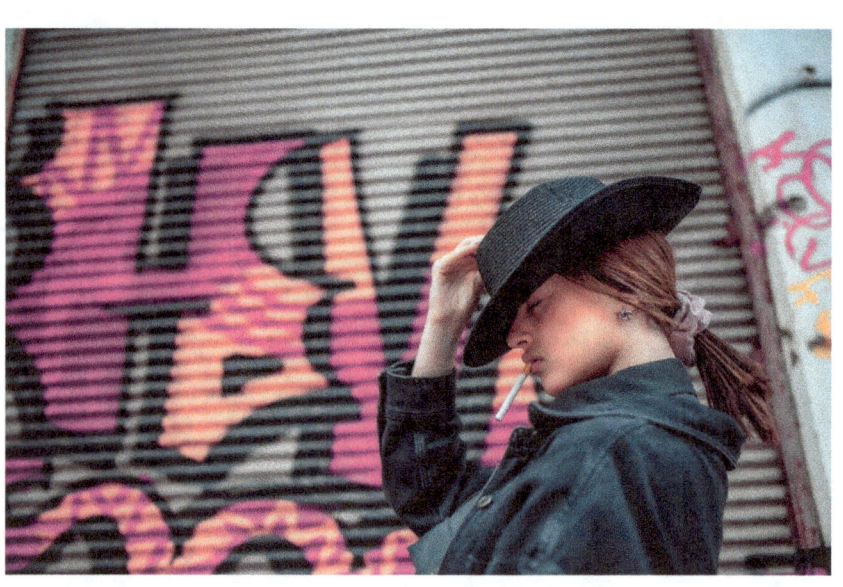

"Photograph: a picture painted
by the sun without instruction
in art."
— Ambrose Bierce

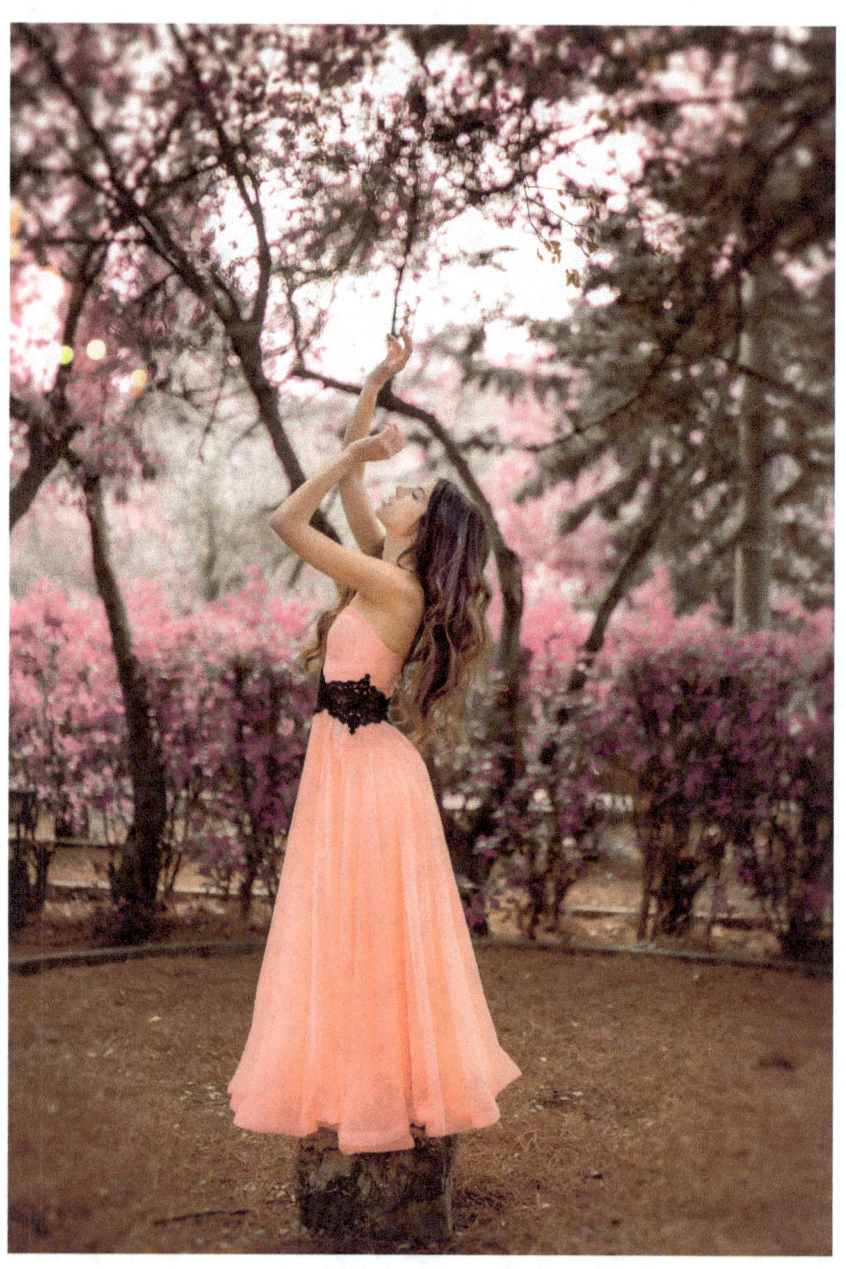

"Every artist has a central story to tell, and the difficulty, the impossible task, is trying to present that story in pictures."
— Gregory Crewdson

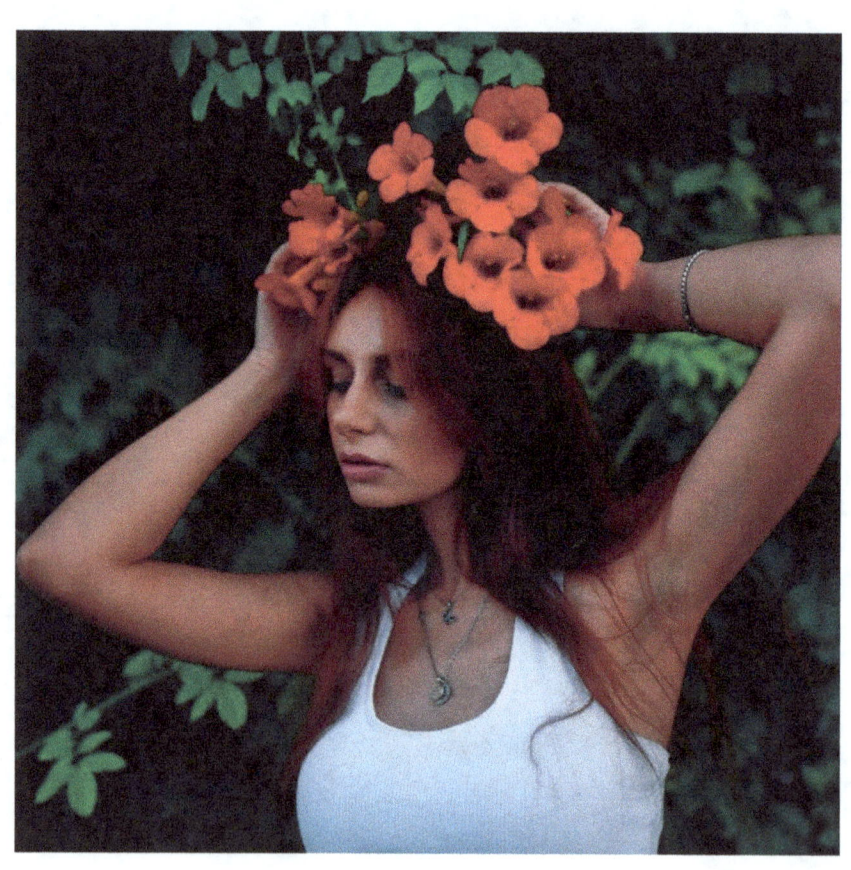

"Photography is truth."
— Jean-Luc Godard

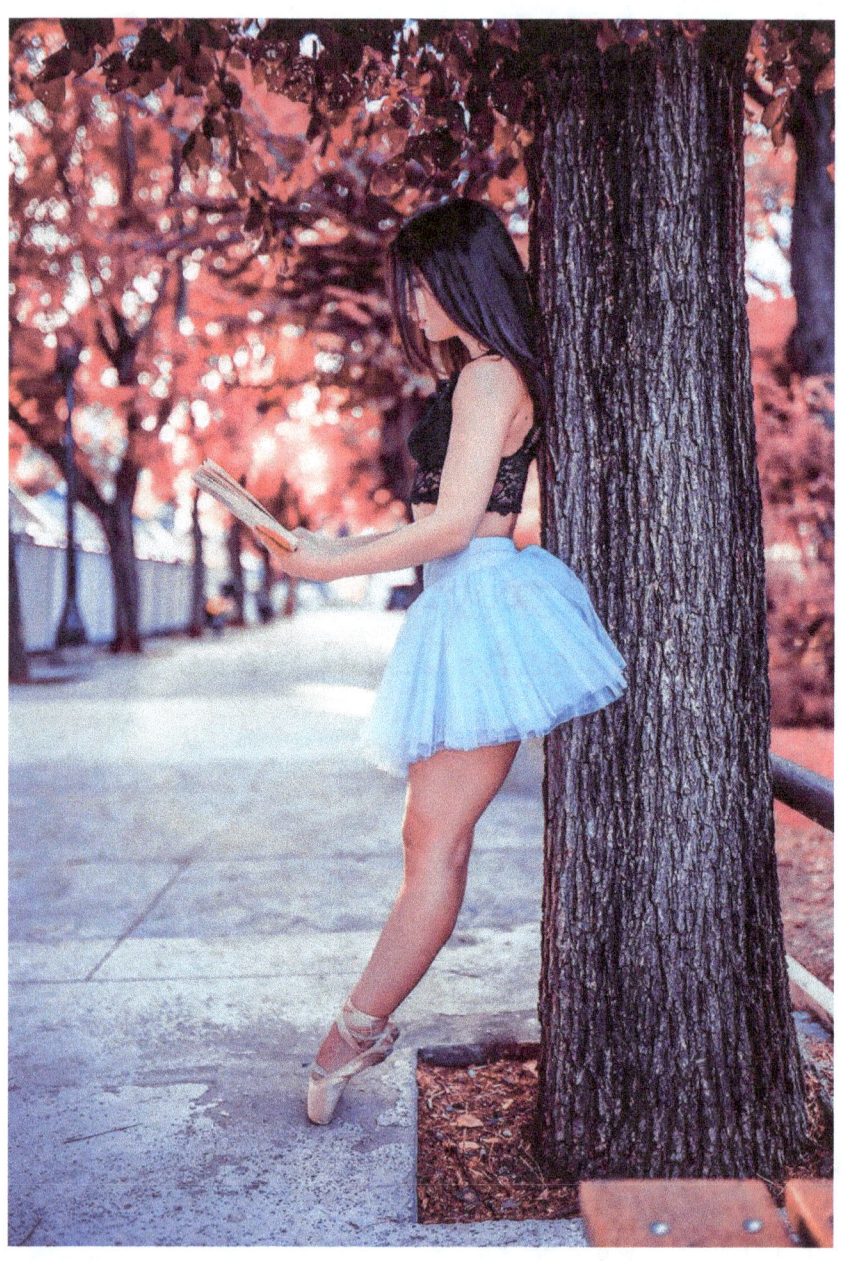

"Photographers mistake the emotion they feel while taking the photo as a judgment that the photograph is good."
— Garry Winogrand

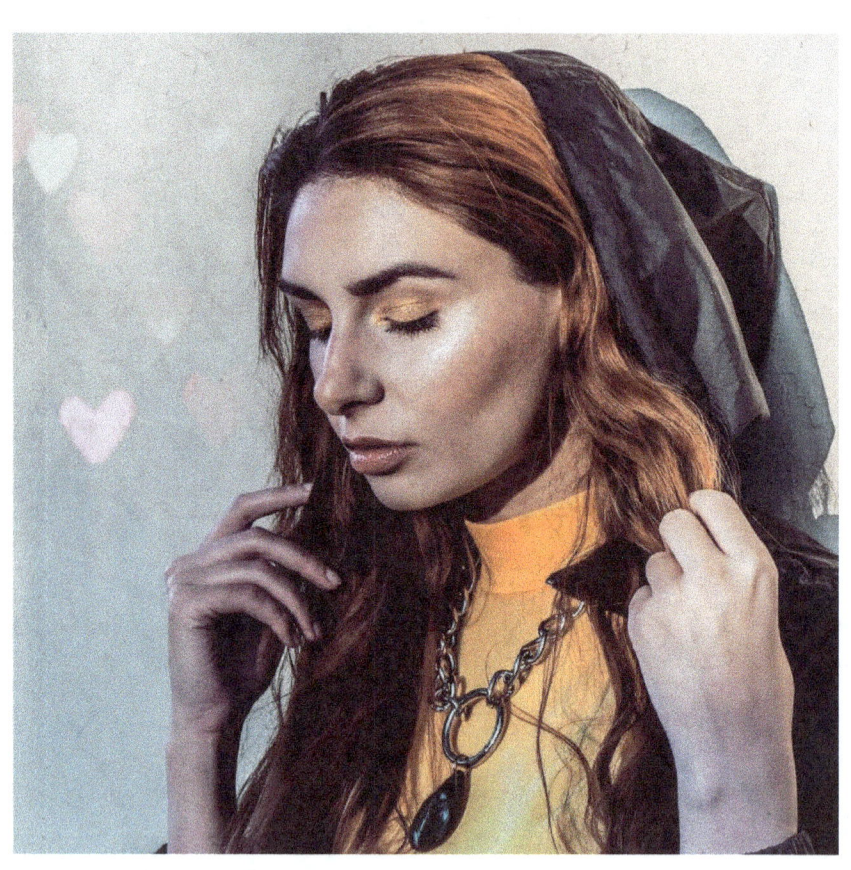

"Photography can only represent the present. Once photographed, the subject becomes part of the past."
— Berenice Abbott

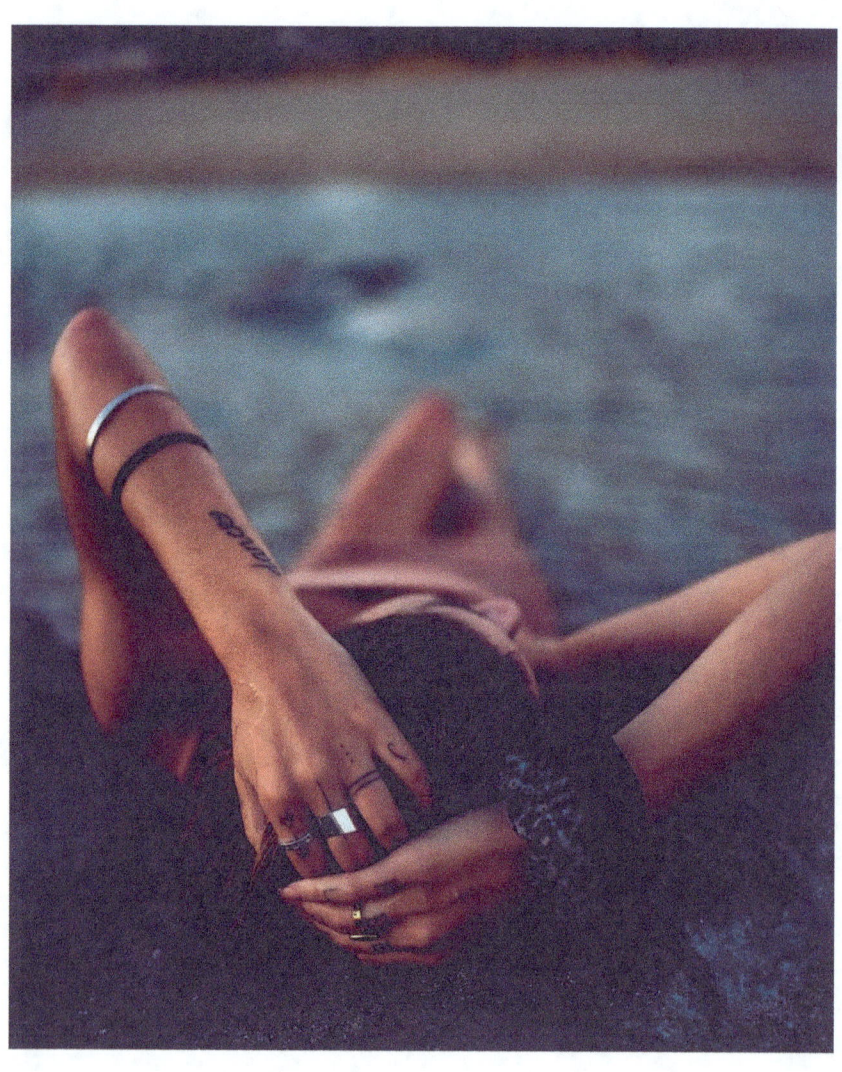

"Photography has nothing to do
with cameras."
— Lucas Gentry

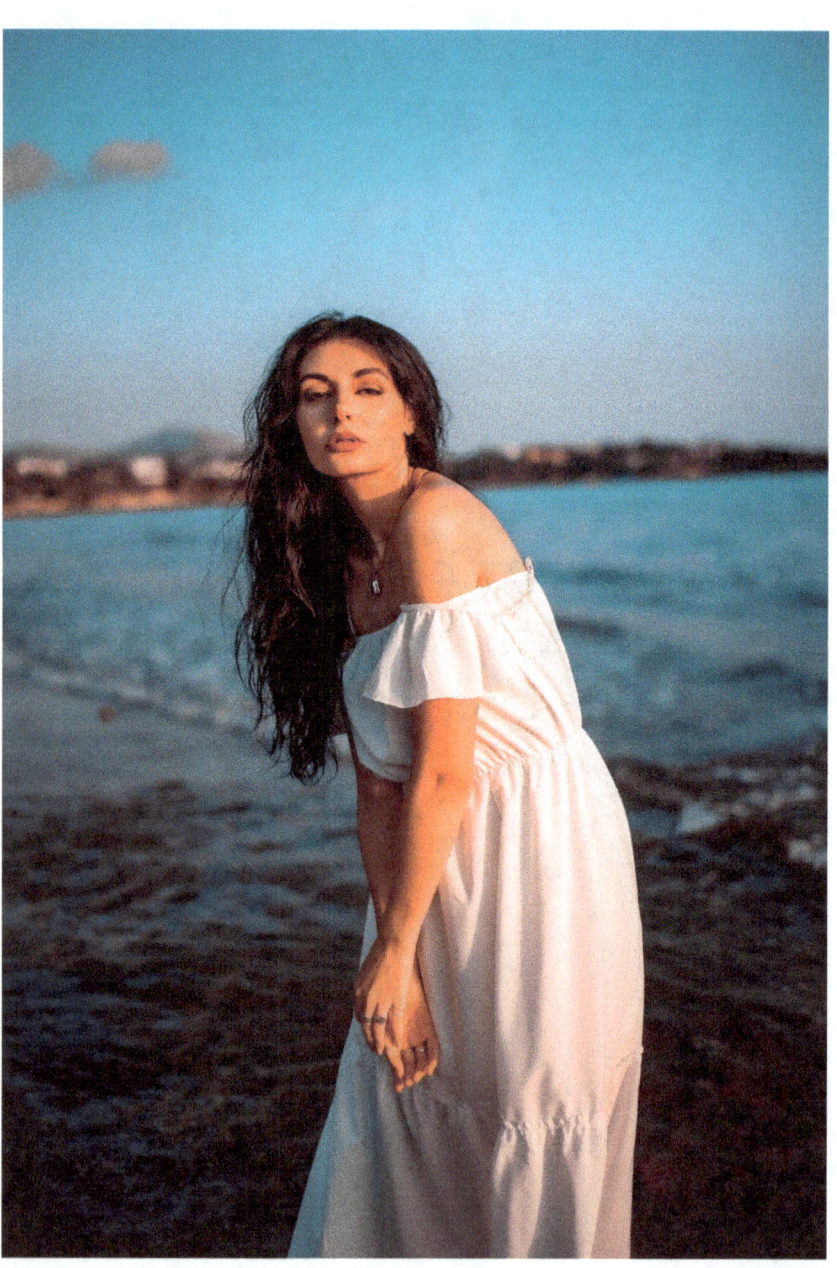

"The more pictures you see, the better you are as a photographer."
— Robert Mapplethorpe

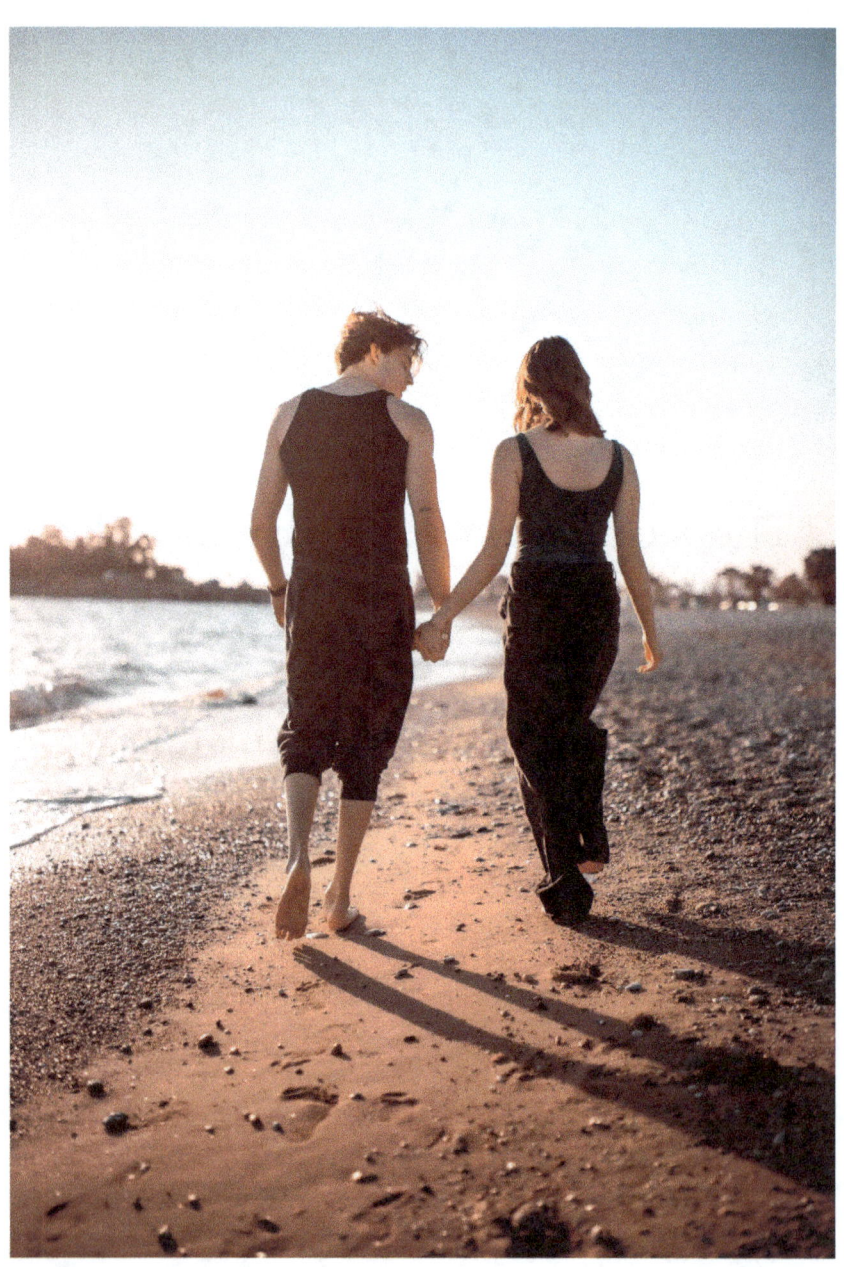

"I am not interested in shooting new things – I am interested to see things new."
— Ernst Haas

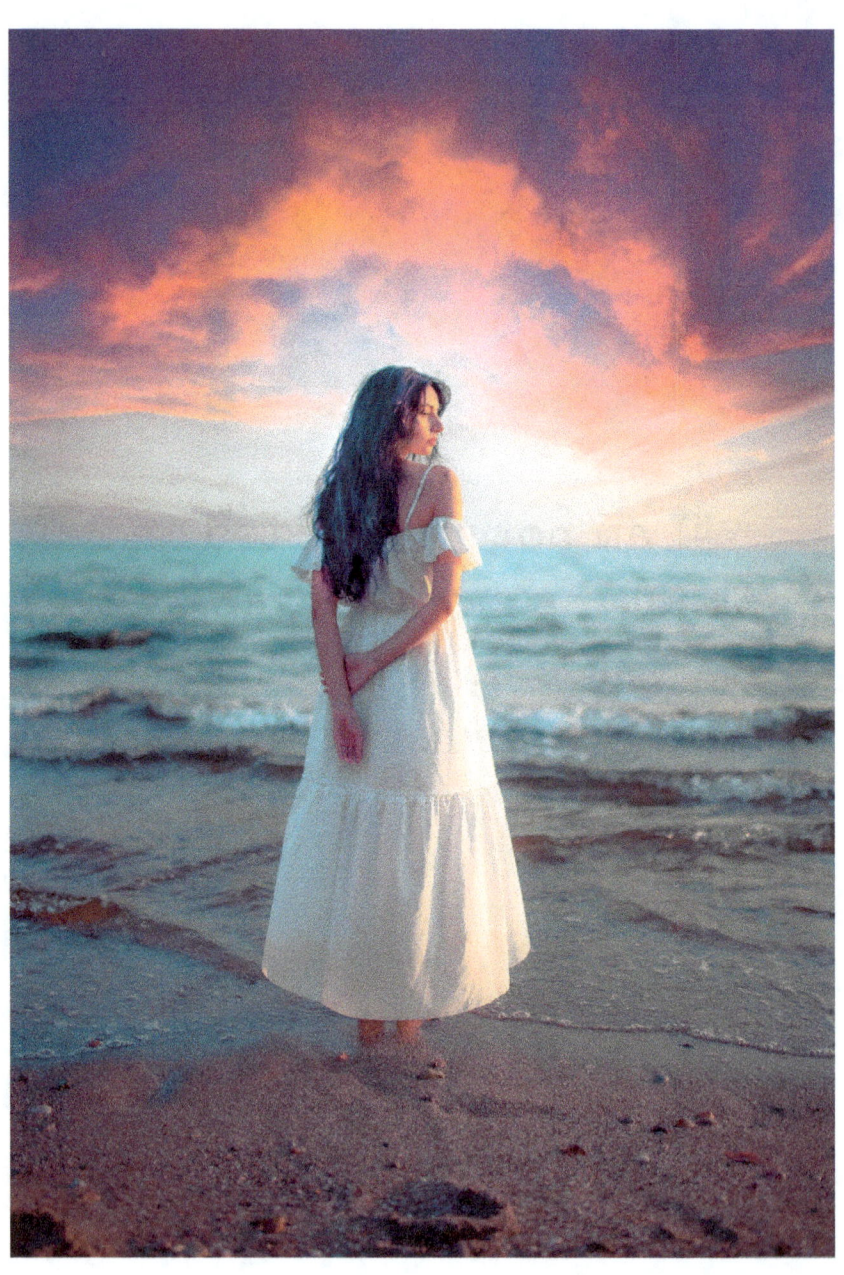

"A photograph is a secret about a secret. The more it tells you the less you know."
— Diane Arbus

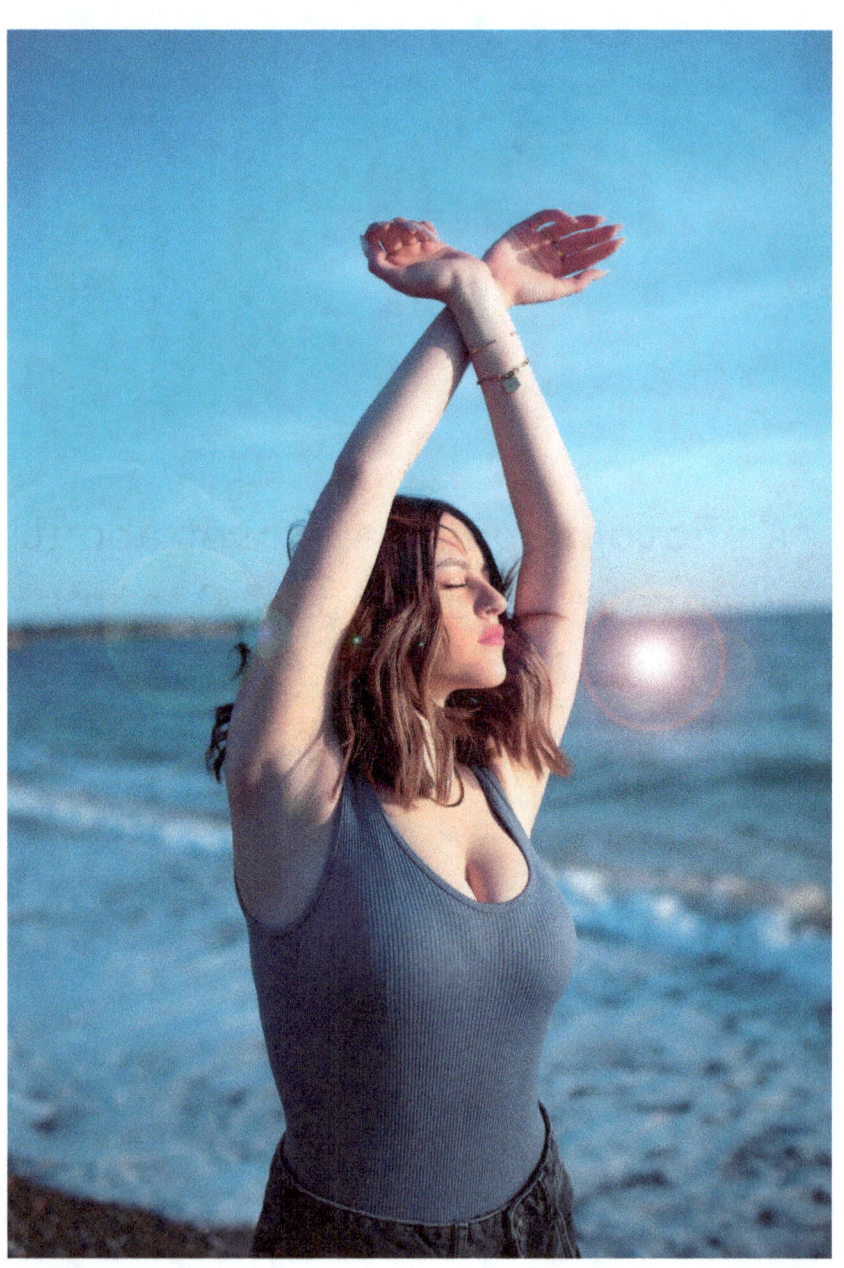

"If you are out there shooting, things will happen for you. If you're not out there, you'll only hear about it."
— Jay Maisel

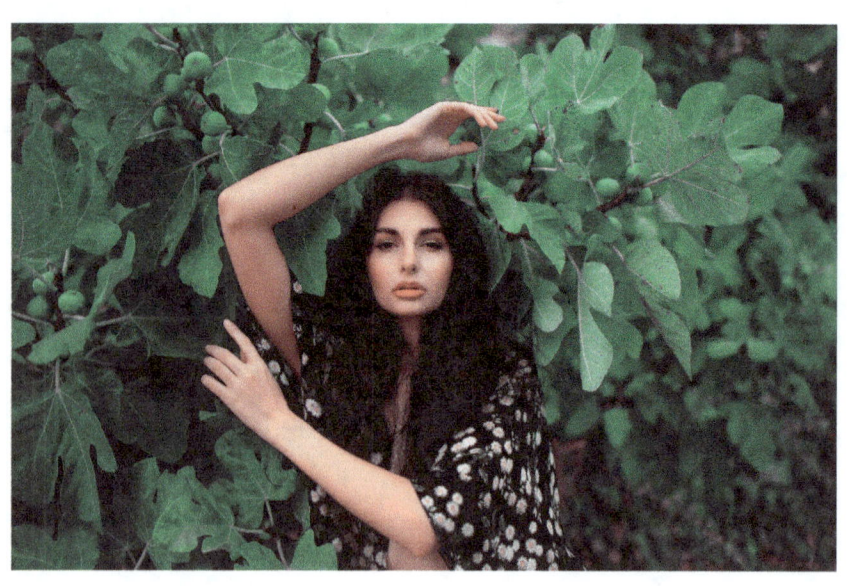

"It is an illusion that photos are made with the camera... they are made with the eye, heart and head."
— Henri Cartier-Bresson

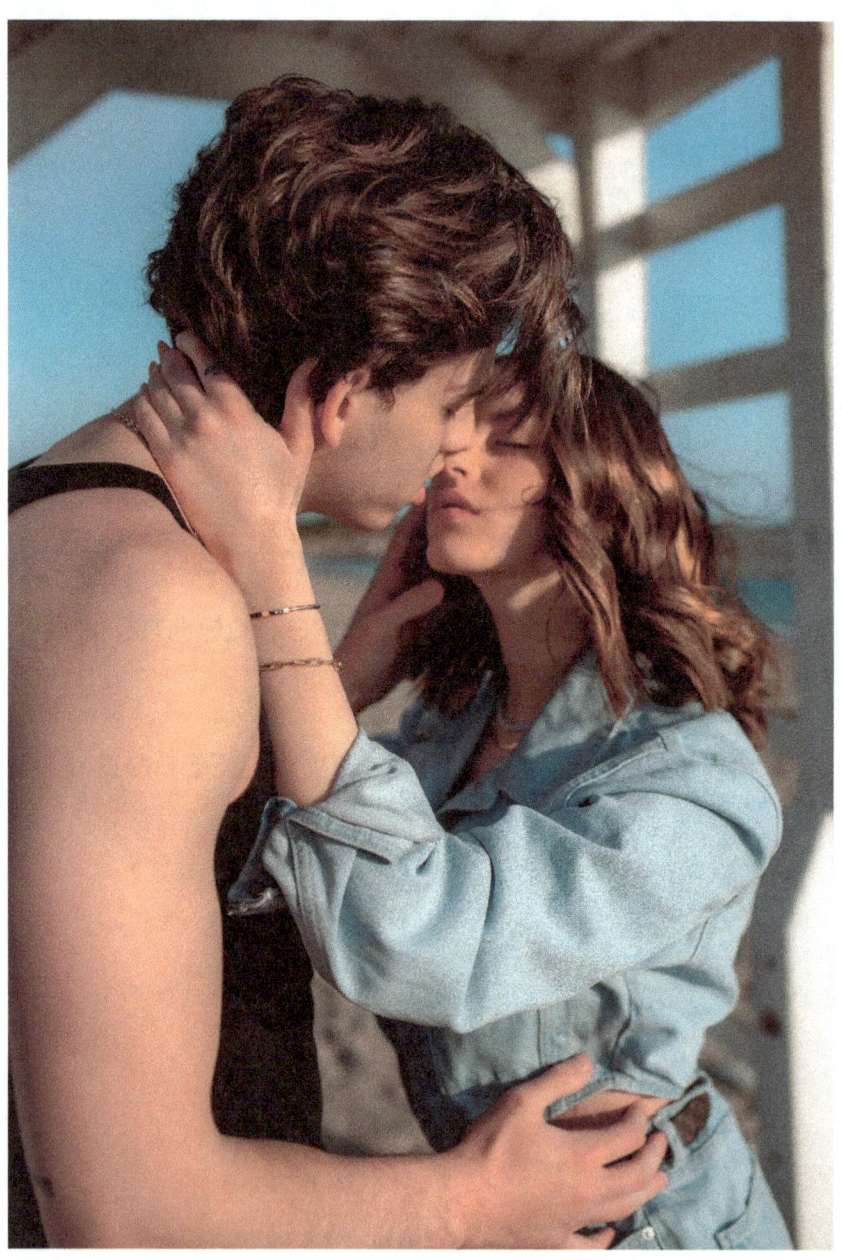

"The whole point of taking pictures is so that you don't have to explain things with words."
— Elliott Erwitt

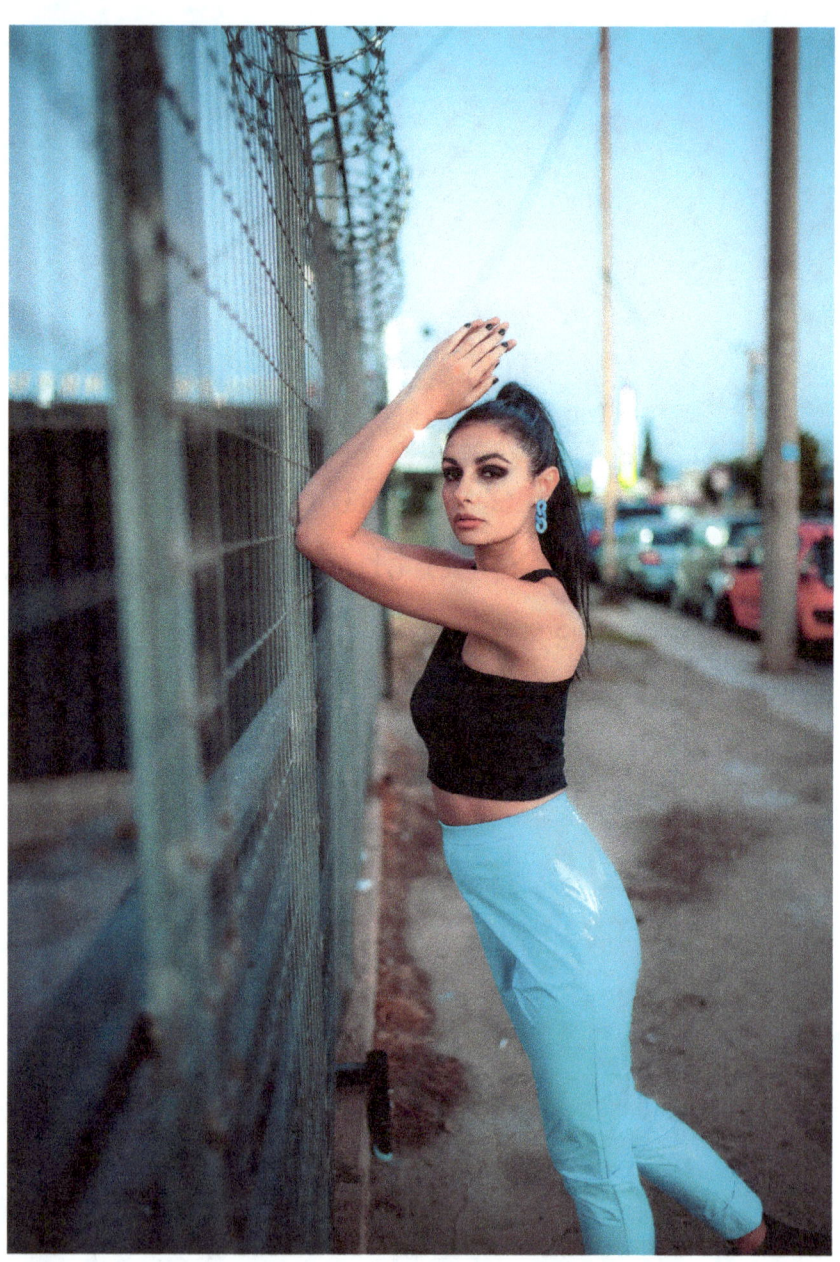

"Photography takes an instant
out of time, altering life by
holding it still."
— Dorothea Lange

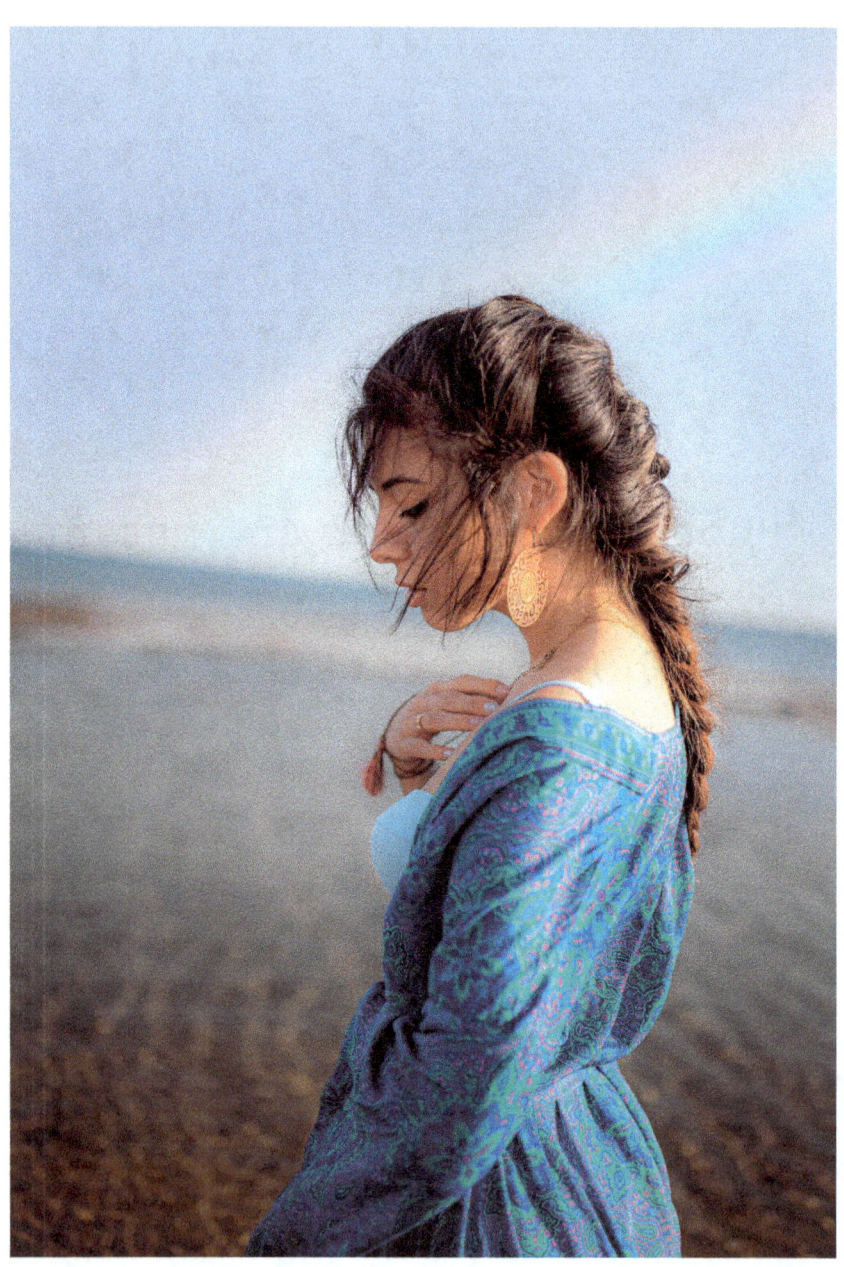

"What I like about photographs
is that they capture a moment
that's gone forever, impossible
to reproduce."
— Karl Lagerfeld

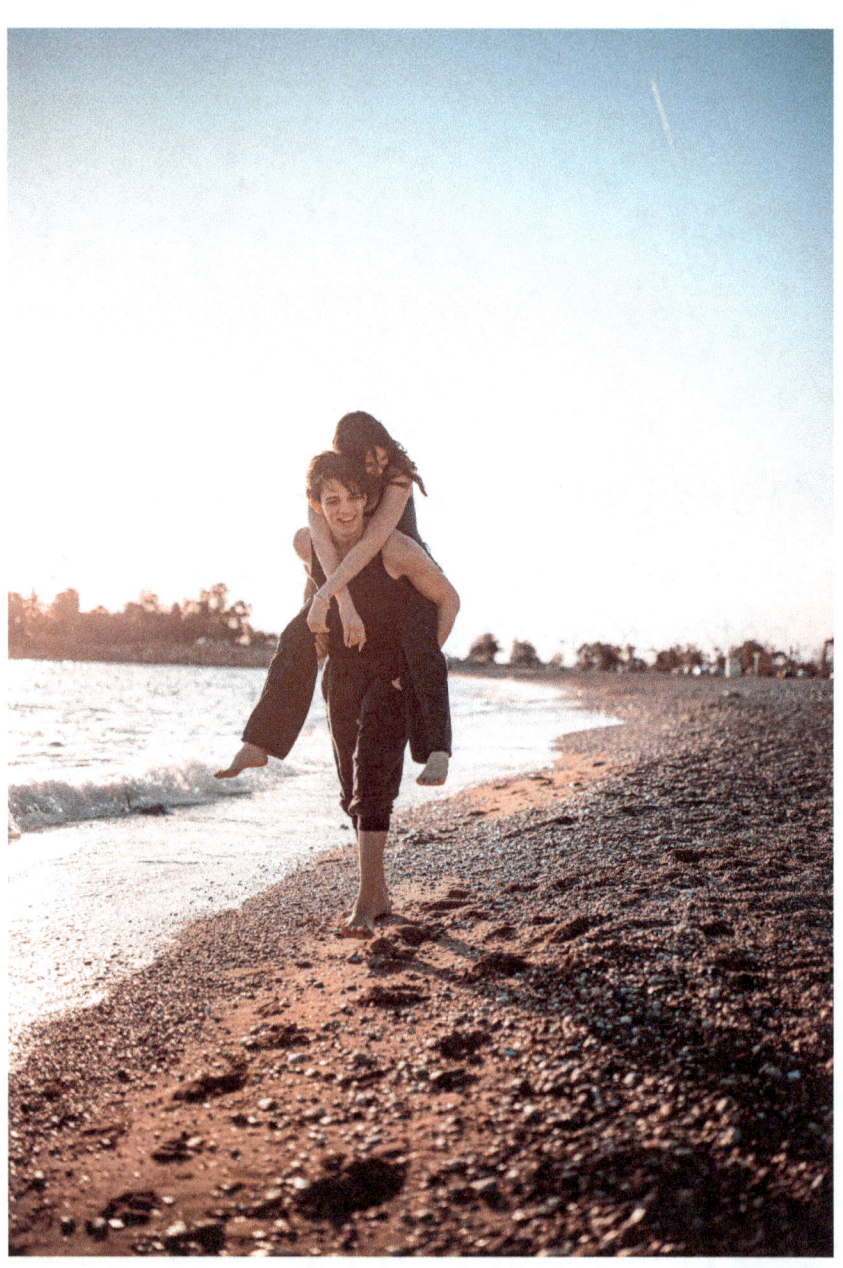

"There is only you and your
camera. The limitations in your
photography are in yourself,
for what we see is what we are."
— Ernst Haas

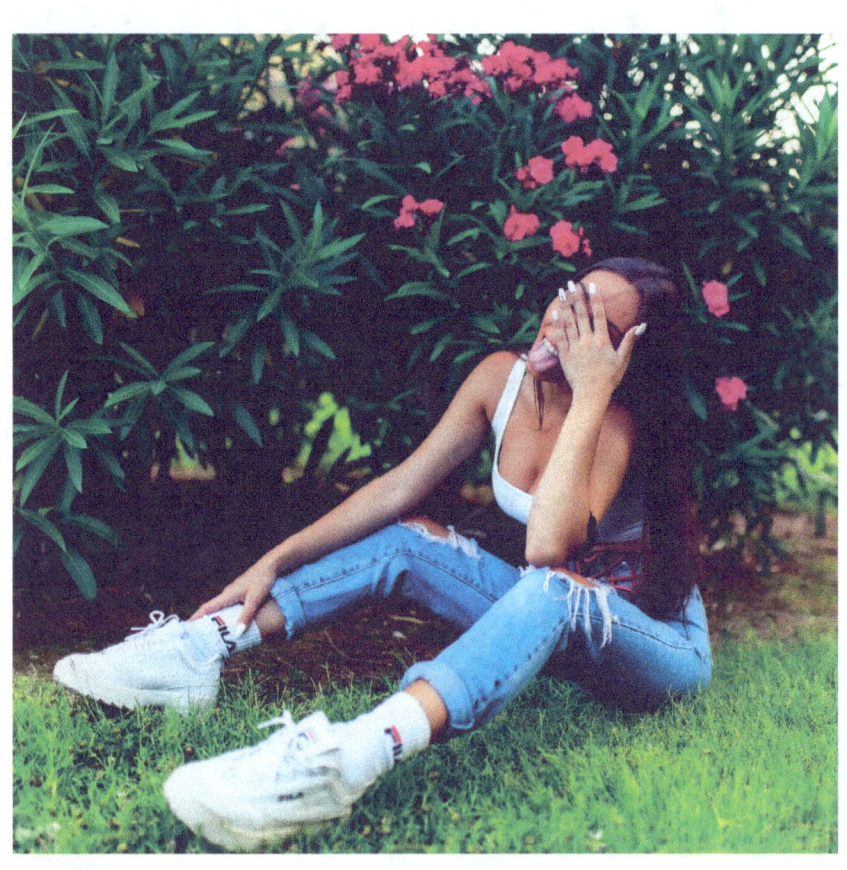

"Wherever there is light, one
can photograph."
— Alfred Stieglitz

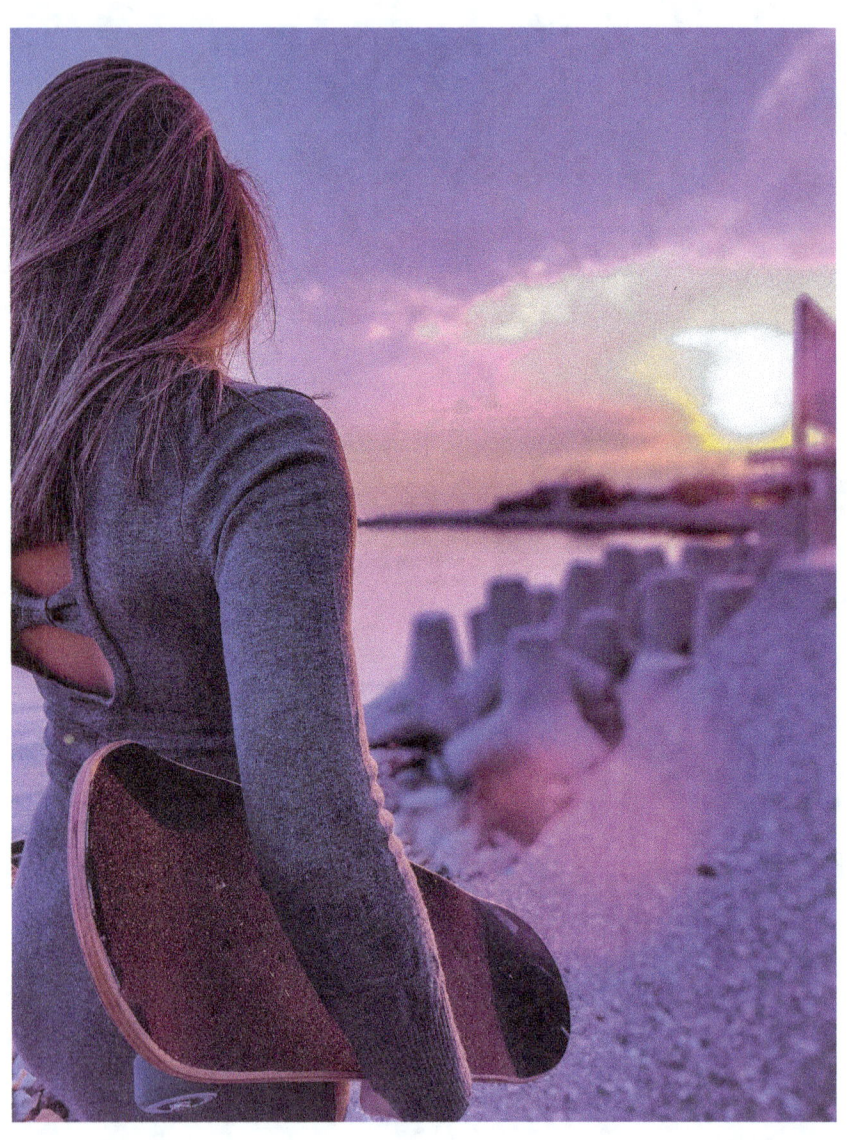

"Since I'm inarticulate, I express myself with images."
— Helen Levitt

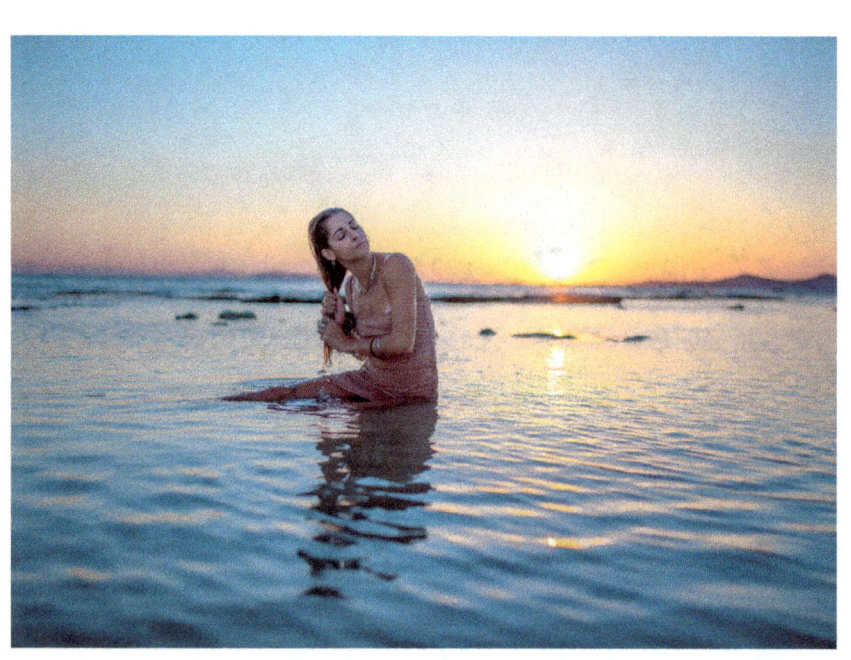

"Beauty can be seen in all things, seeing and composing the beauty is what separates the snapshot from the photograph."
— Matt Hardy

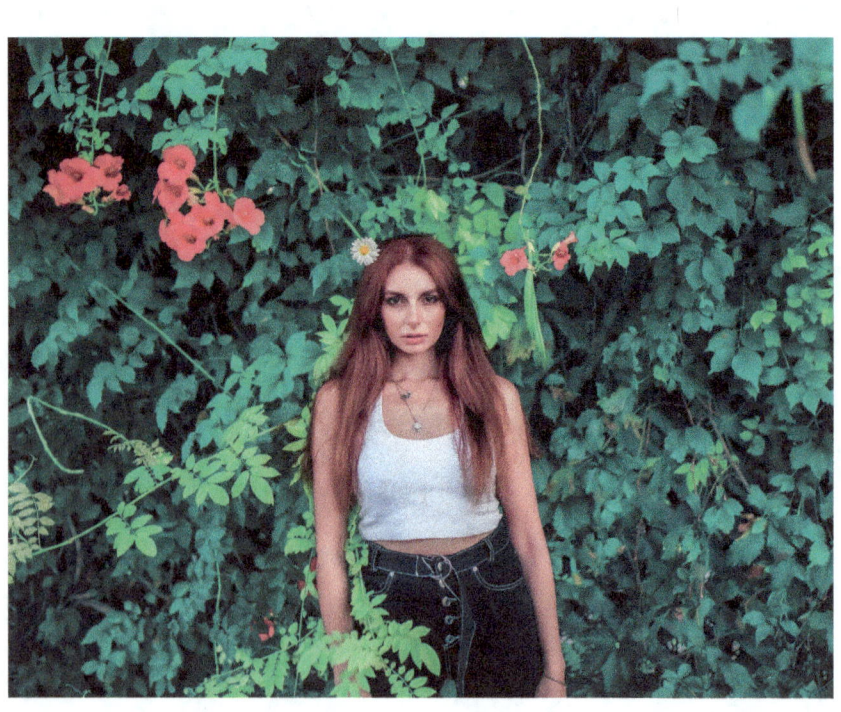

"You don't take a photograph,
you make it."
— Ansel Adams

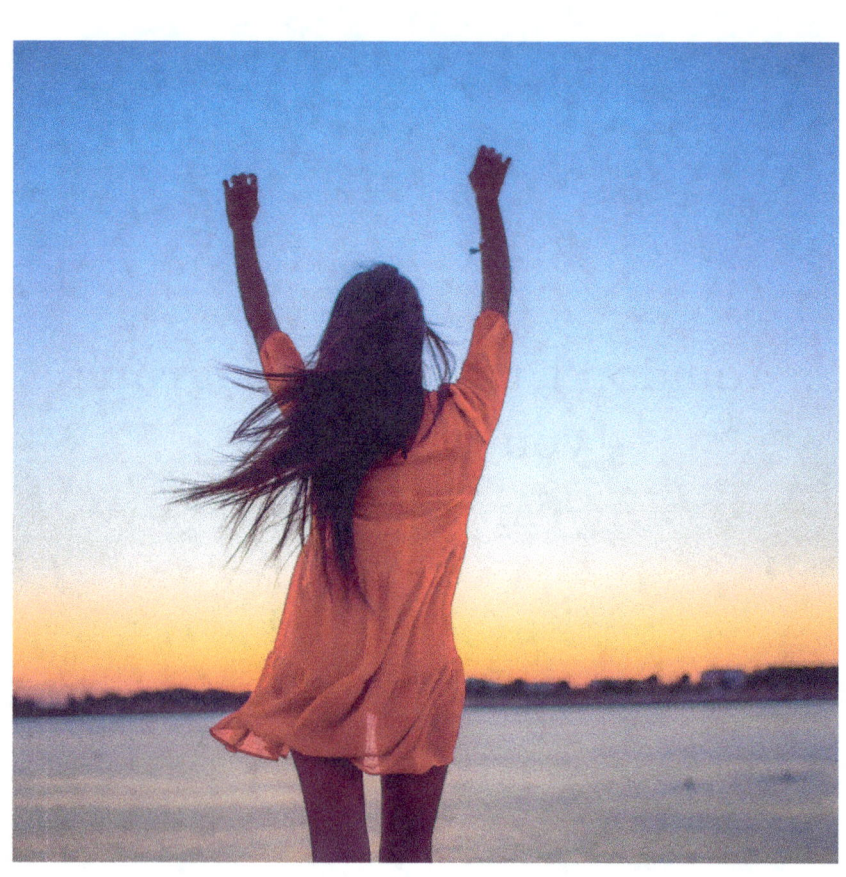

"With photography, I like to create a fiction out of reality. I try and do this by taking society's natural prejudice and giving this a twist."
— Martin Parr

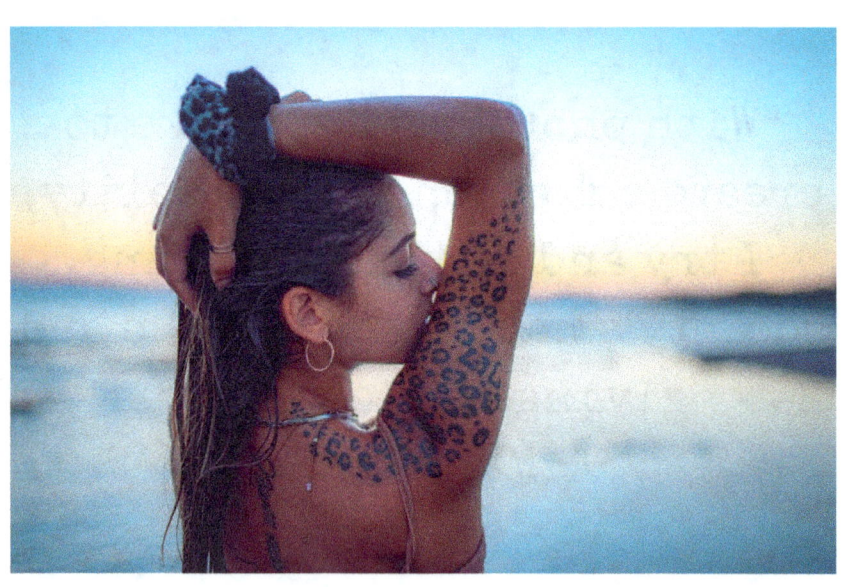

"When people ask me what equipment I use – I tell them my eyes."
— Anonymous

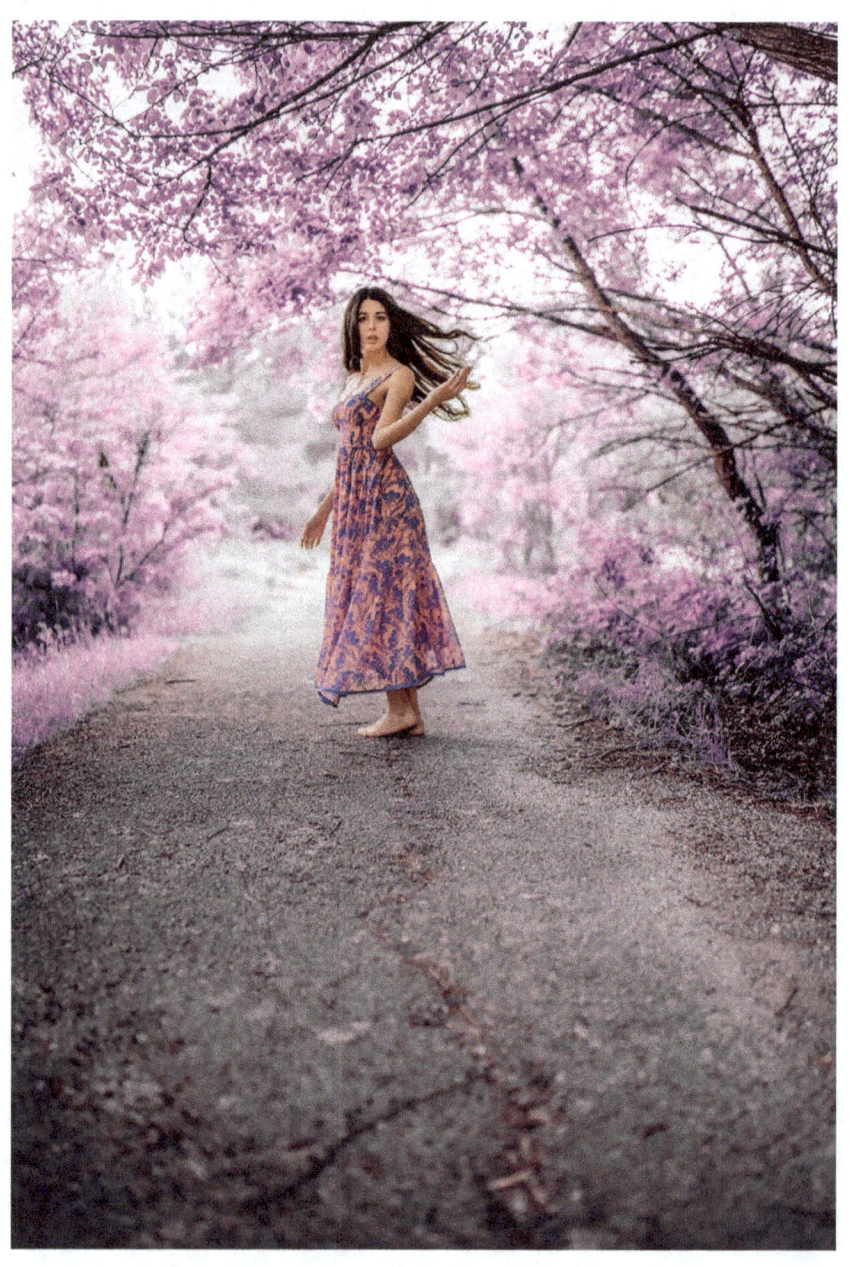

"Photography is the simplest
thing in the world, but it is
incredibly complicated to make
it really work."
— Martin Parr

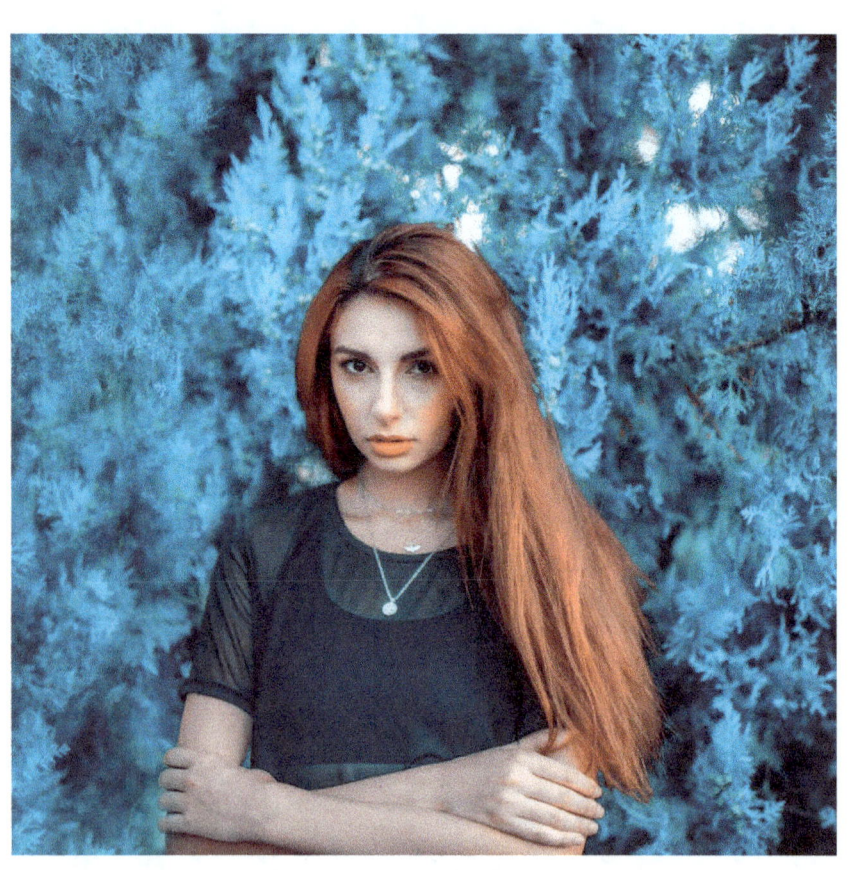

"All photographs are accurate.
None of them is the truth."
— Richard Avedon

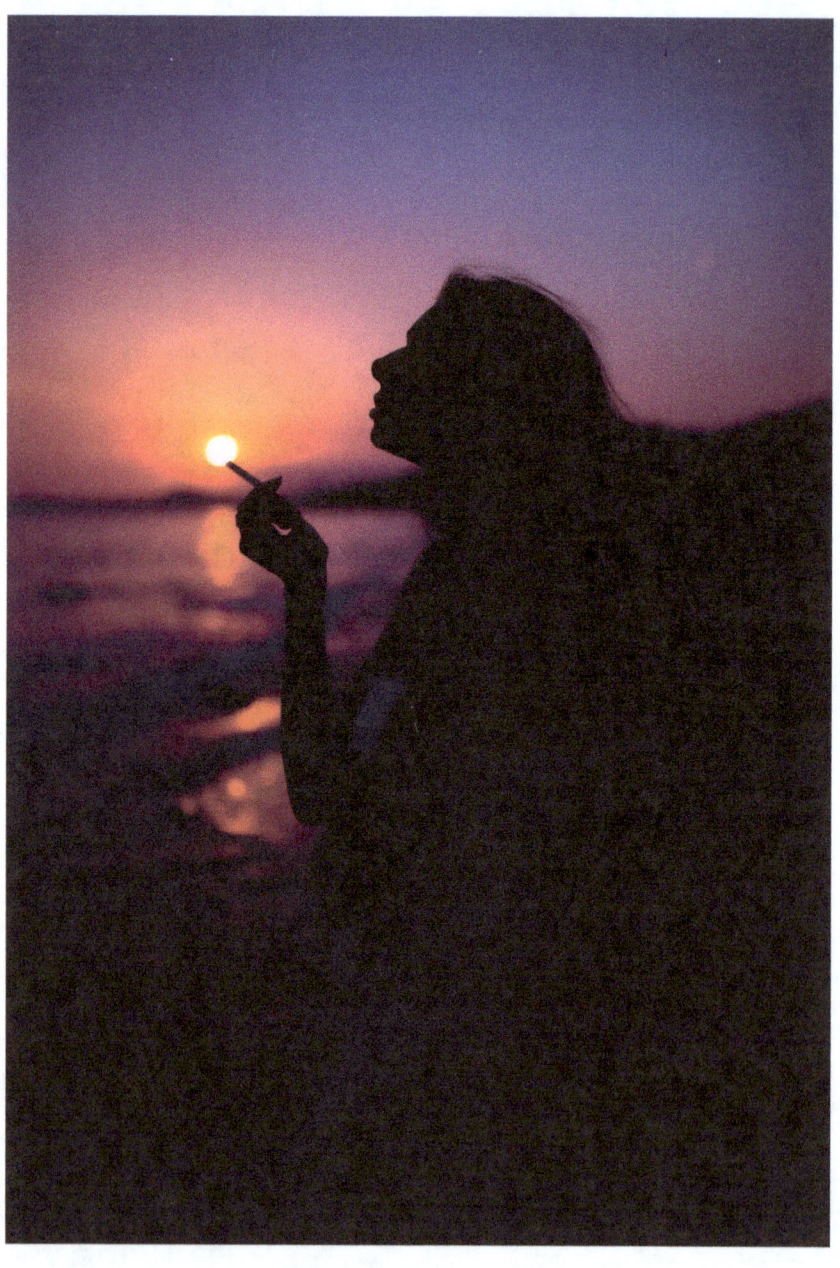

"You can look at a picture for a week and never think of it again. You can also look at the picture for a second and think of it all your life."
— Joan Miro

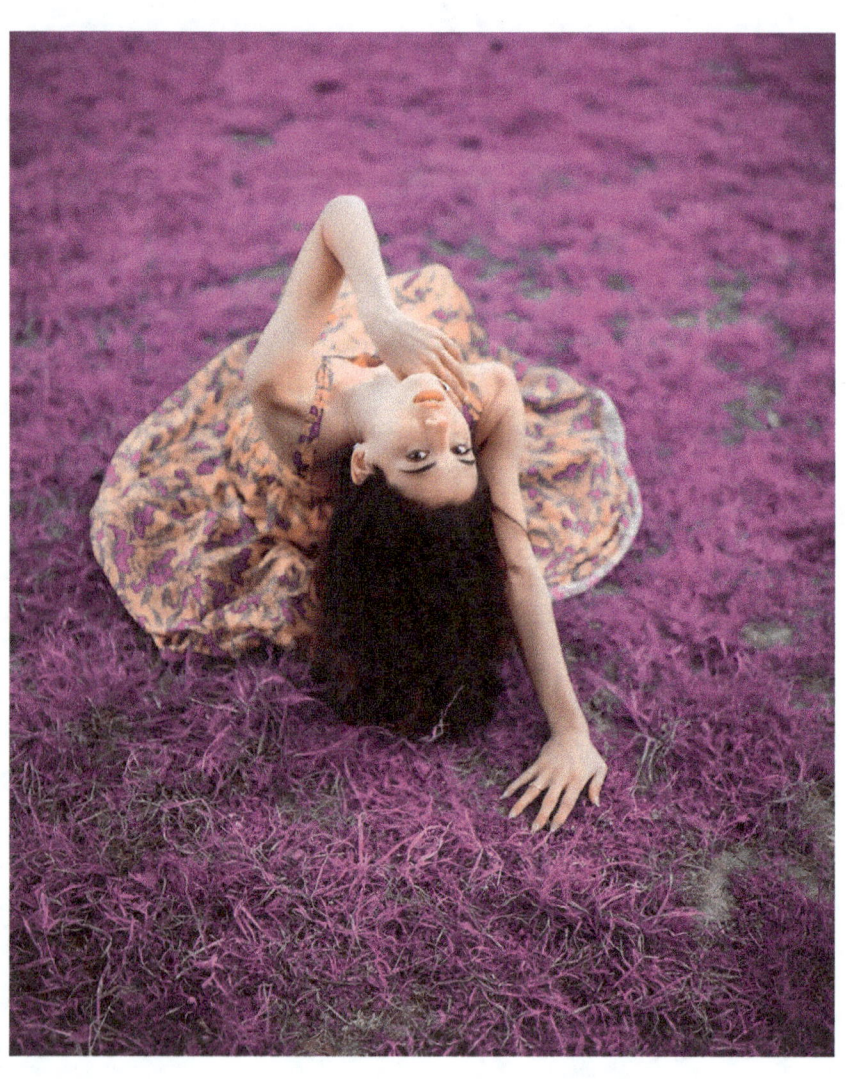

"Photography is about finding out what can happen in the frame. When you put four edges around some facts, you change those facts."
— Garry Winogrand

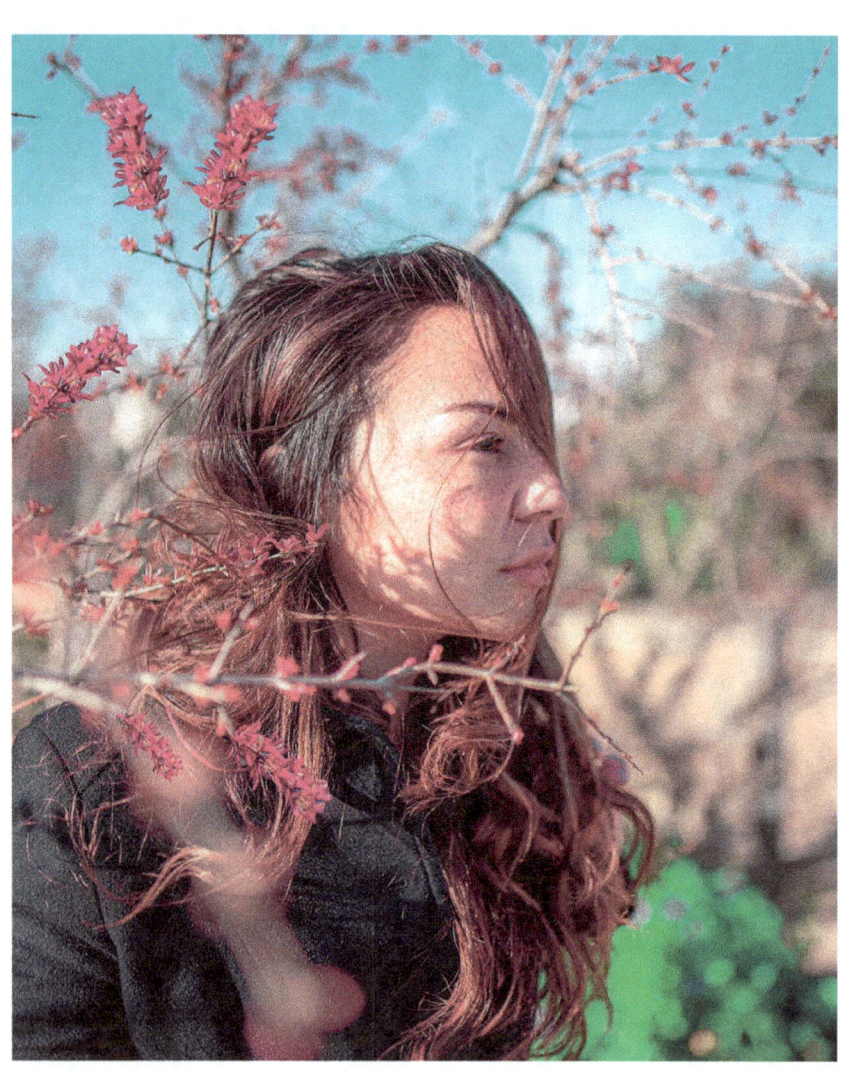

"Light makes photography. Embrace light. Admire it. Love it. But above all, know light. Know it for all you are worth, and you will know the key to photography."
— George Eastman

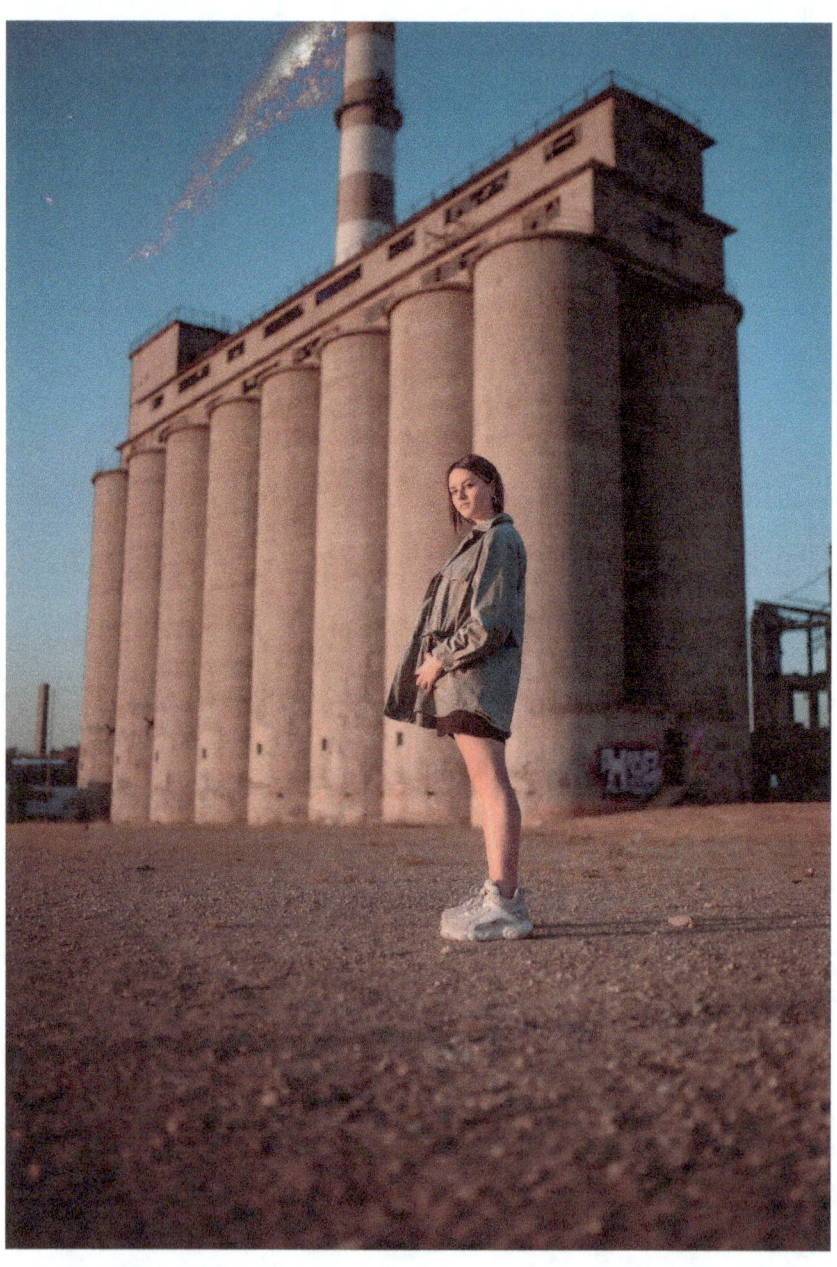

"I think good dreaming is what
leads to good photographs."
— Wayne Miller

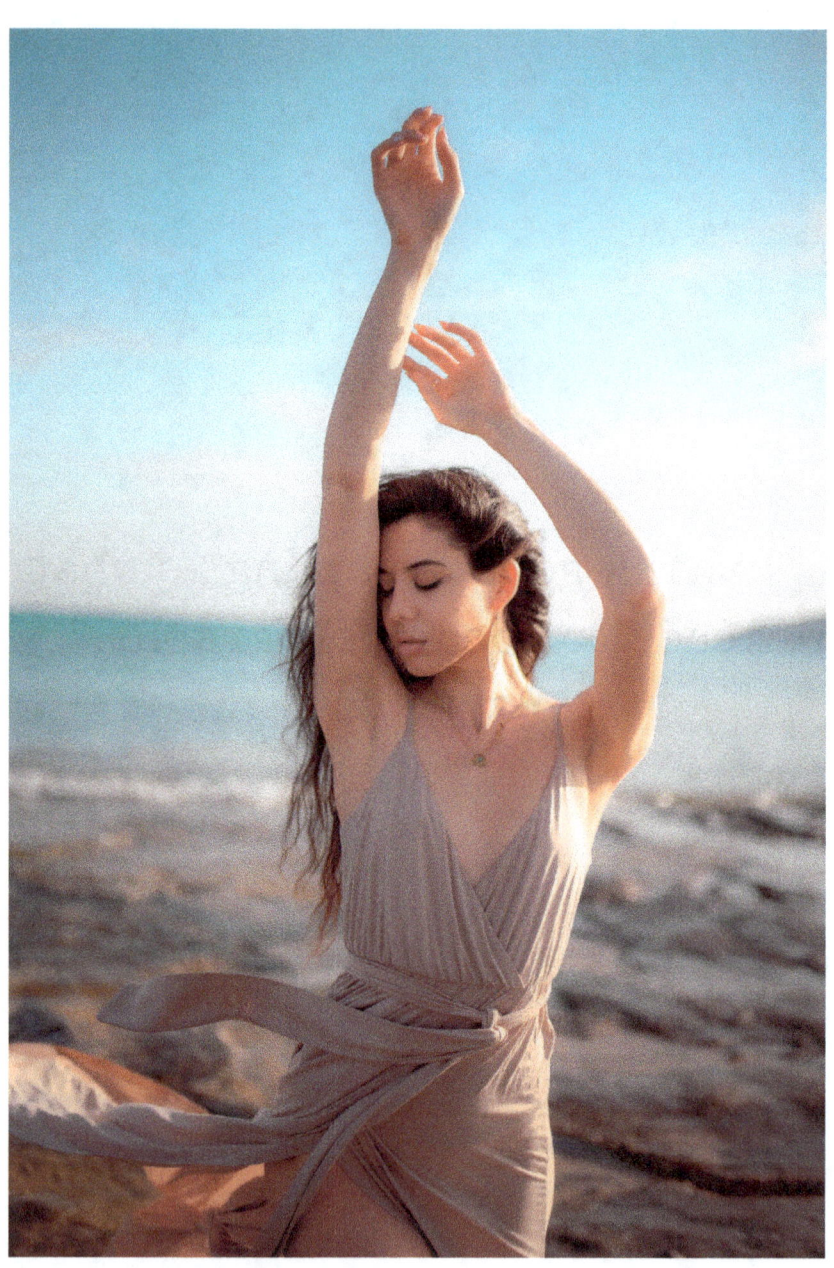

"I love the people I photograph.
I mean, they're my friends. I've
never met most of them or I don't
know them at all, yet through my
images I live with them."
— Bruce Gilden

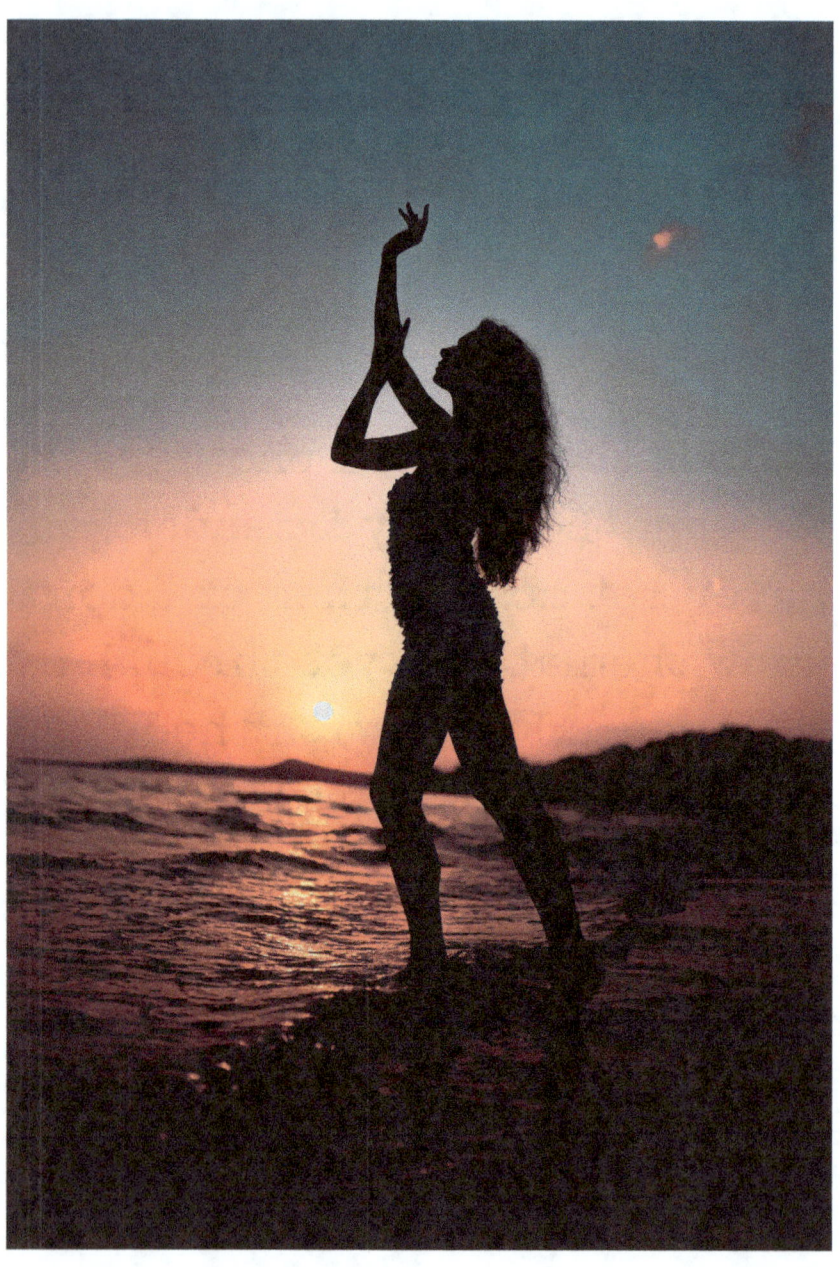

"To photograph is to hold one's breath, when all faculties converge to capture fleeting reality. It's at that precise moment that mastering an image becomes a great physical and intellectual joy."
— Henri Cartier-Bresson

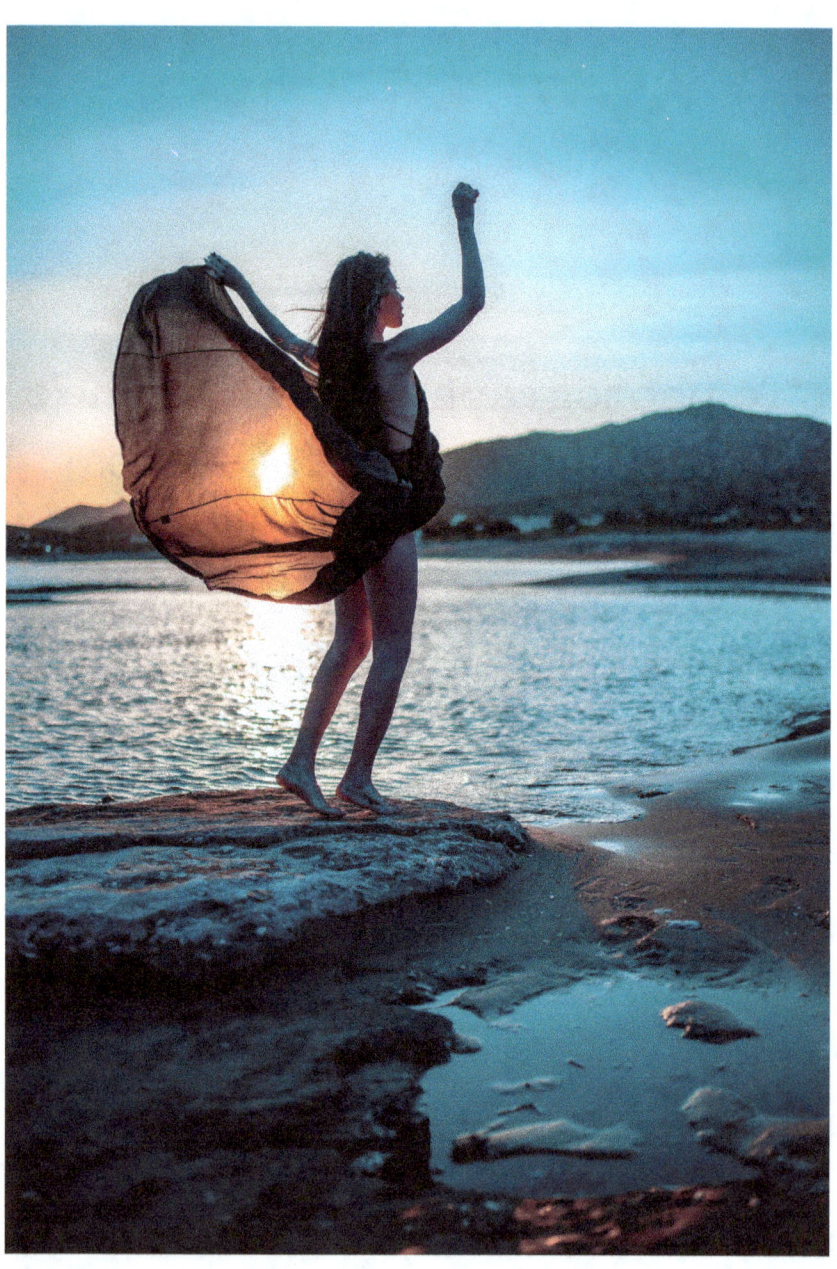

"Taking pictures is savoring
life intensely every hundredth
of a second."
— Marc Riboud

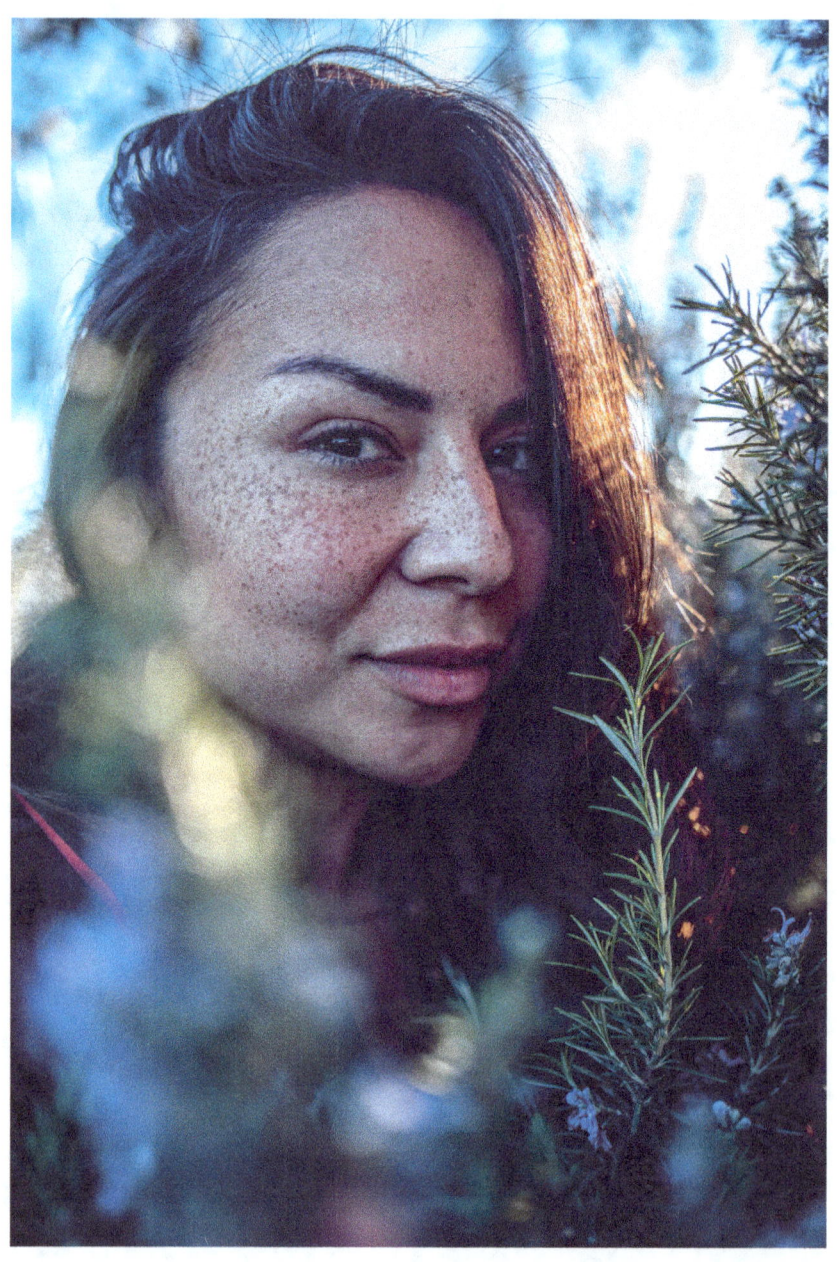

"When I say I want to photograph someone, what it really means is that I'd like to know them. Anyone I know I photograph."
— Annie Leibovitz

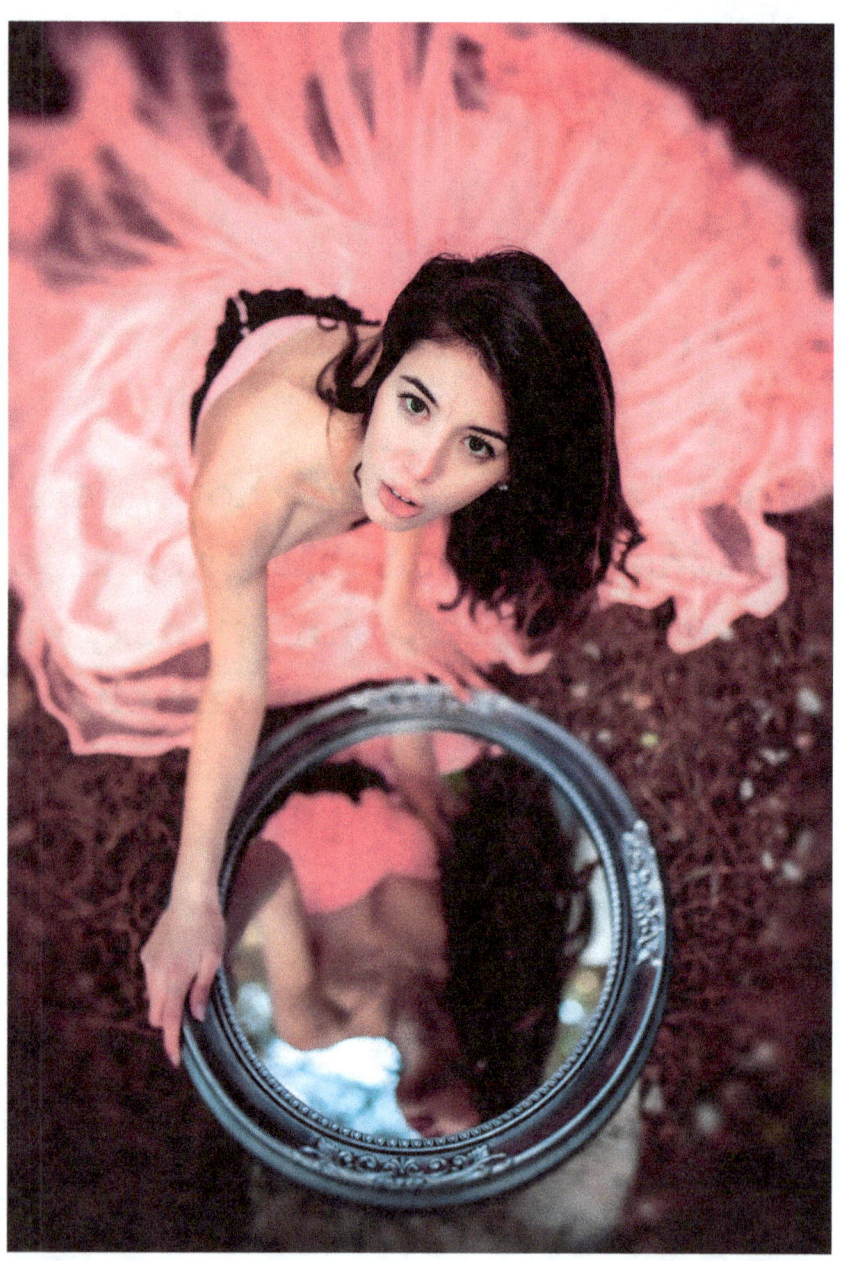

"Look and think before opening the shutter. The heart and mind are the true lens of the camera."
— Yousuf Karsh

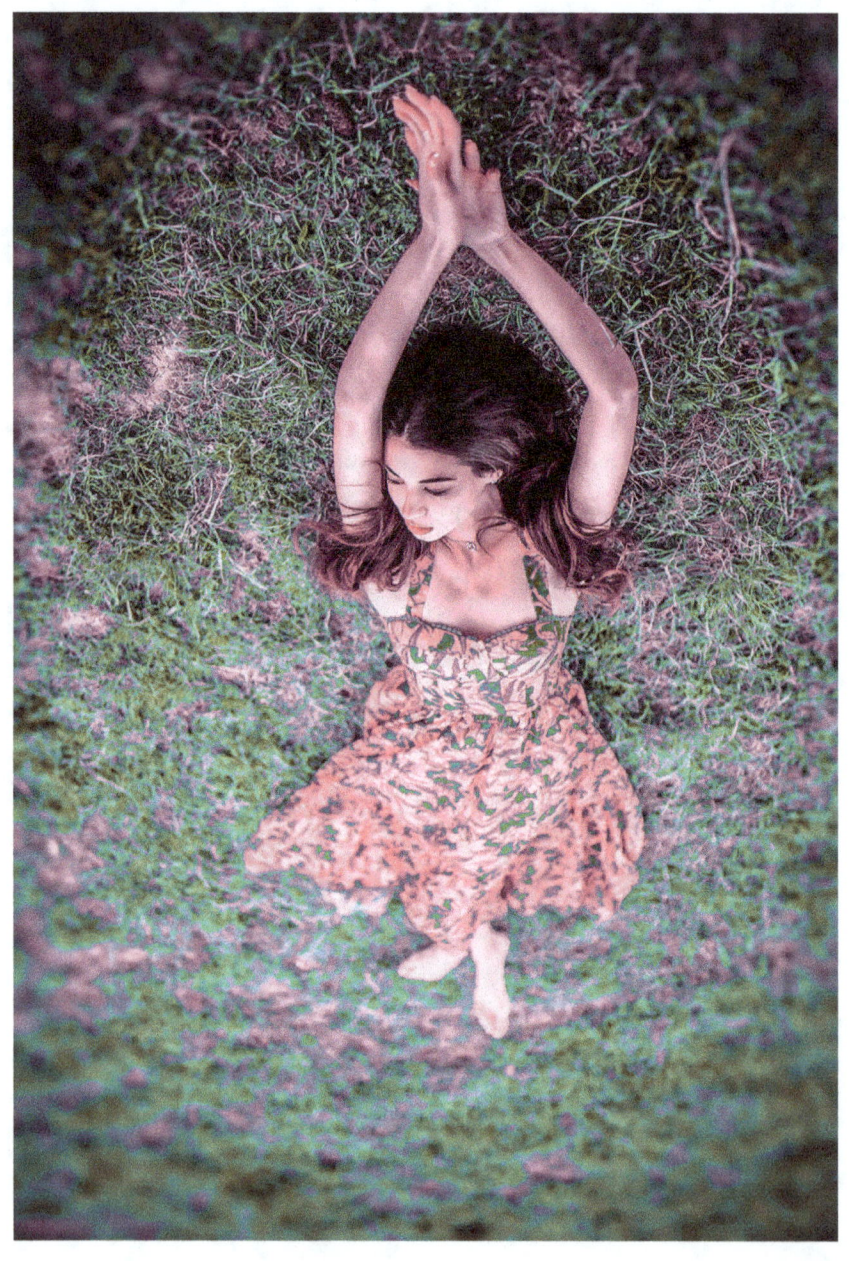

As we come to the final pages of "The Magic Tales: Portraits of Enchantment," I am reminded of the incredible journey we've shared through the lens of a camera. This collection of photographs has been a labor of love, a testament to the beauty of our world, the stories of its people, and the enchantment that exists within us all.

From the very beginning, the aim of this book was to capture not just moments, but emotions, dreams, and the intricate threads that bind us together as human beings. It was a journey of discovery, where each click of the camera shutter unraveled a new chapter in the book of life.

The portraits within these pages are more than just images; they are reflections of the lives and experiences of countless individuals, each with their own unique story. These faces, expressions, and moments have allowed us to glimpse the shared humanity that transcends time and place.

I am grateful for the opportunity to have shared these stories with you, to have transported you to the enchanting worlds captured in these frames. Photography is a powerful medium that enables us to freeze time, yet it also has the power to unfreeze our hearts, allowing us to connect with the world and the people in it on a deeper level.

As you have journeyed with me through these photographs, I hope you have found inspiration, wonder, and perhaps a touch of magic. I hope you've been reminded that in every face, there is a story, in every moment, there is beauty, and in every glance, there is connection.

Before we part ways, I would like to share one more piece of information. All the photographs in this book were taken between 2018 and 2023. They are a snapshot of this five-year journey, a testament to the evolving nature of life and the beauty that can be found in each passing year.

Thank you for embarking on this visual adventure with me. I hope these "Magic Tales" continue to inspire you to seek out enchantment in your own life, to find stories within the faces you encounter, and to capture the magic of the world around you.

With heartfelt gratitude,

Nickos IV
03/09/2023 - Piraeus, Greece

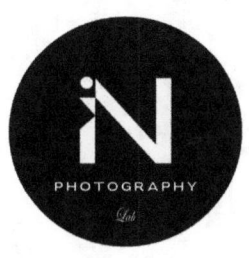

www.ivphotographylab.com

1st Edition
09/2023
Athens

-Nickos IV-

www.ingramcontent.com/pod-product-compliance
Lightning Source LLC
Chambersburg PA
CBHW072324290526
45794CB00002B/741